SOWING THE SEED

A

Sowing the Seed

Selections from 'The Sower'

edited by Francis Somerville SJ

 St Paul Publications

ST PAUL PUBLICATIONS
SLOUGH   SL3 6BT   ENGLAND

Nihil obstat: John Barton, censor
Imprimatur: + Victor Guazzelli, v.g.
             Westminster, 13 September 1972

The *Nihil obstat* and *Imprimatur* are a declaration that a book or pamphlet is considered to be free from doctrinal or moral error. It is not implied that those who have granted the *Nihil obstat* and *Imprimatur* agree with the contents, opinions or statements expressed.

Printed in Great Britain by the Society of St Paul, Slough
SBN 85439 088 X

Contents

Foreword

"If your lips confess that Jesus is Lord and if you believe in your heart that God raised him from the dead, then you will be saved. By believing from the heart, you are made righteous; by confessing with your lips you are saved. When Scripture says: 'those who believe in him will have no cause for shame', it makes no distinction between Jew and Greek; all belong to the same Lord who is rich enough, however many ask his help, 'for everyone who calls on the Lord will be saved'. But they will not ask his help unless they believe in him, and they will not believe in him unless they have heard of him, and they will not hear of him unless they get a preacher, and they will never have a preacher unless one is sent. . . . So faith comes from what is preached, and what is preached comes from the word of Christ." (Romans 10. 9-17)

What is the Christian religion teacher trying to do when he is teaching religion? More basically one might ask, can one, in fact, teach religion? One can teach *about* religion and religions. But can one really teach religion? Would it not be truer to say that the Christian educator seeks to share with the pupils his faith-experience, his never ending search into the mystery of Christ and the meaning Christ sheds on life today? And the aim of this sharing? Surely, that these young people will gradually become integrated and mature human beings, able to develop good relationships with other people, and be open in their response to God. It is, of course, their response to God which alone helps people, young or old, continually to break out of their prison of egocentricity. It is God alone whose Spirit will lead people to become 'men for others' after the manner of the One whose name they profess. 'He who follows Christ, the perfect Man, becomes himself more human', says a Vatican II decree. Christian educators are agents of the Spirit in this work of humanization, the indispensable prelude to christianization.

A few years ago Roman Catholic educators might have been forgiven for regarding the changes in religion teaching as a passing fashion. Transition is almost endemic to education. 'If we only wait long enough', some teachers might have been tempted to say, 'the dust will settle, and we shall find that the religion "lessons" we received as pupils ourselves and later gave as teachers, are back in vogue again. As it was in the beginning. . . .'

One hopes that the General Catechetical Directory issued from Rome in April 1971 will have exorcised that ghost. Here are a few quotations from this important document.

'Some renewal in evangelization is needed for transmitting the same faith to new generations. It should be noted that the Christian faith requires explanation and new forms of expression so that it may take root in all successive cultures'.

'Though the aspirations and basic needs peculiar to human nature and the human condition remain essentially the same, nevertheless men of our era are posing new questions about the meaning and importance of life.'

'Believers of our time are certainly not in all respects like believers of the past. That is why it becomes necessary to affirm the permanence of the faith and to present the message of salvation in renewed ways.'

'To be selected in preference to the others are those formulas which, while expressing faithfully the truth of the faith, are adapted to the capacity of the listeners.'

Clearly we are asked to do much more than 'tinker about' with bits and pieces of the Christian message. We need to rethink, not to discard but in order to deepen. We need to deepen our understanding of almost all the Christian mysteries; God, Jesus Christ, the role of the Spirit, prayer and worship, the Church, the Eucharist, penance.

These are some of the subjects dealt with in this book of essays taken from *The Sower*. Canon Drinkwater, that great father of catechetics in the English-speaking world, was the creator of this magazine. Its issues have spanned half a century, fifty years that have marked a revolution in religion teaching. Father Somerville has been the editor for the last twelve years. The essays contained in this compilation are thought-provoking. Not everyone will agree with all the views expressed. There are certainly some opinions which I for one would like to discuss further with their authors. Nevertheless, I believe this book will open-up new theological vistas, and lead the reader to delve more deeply into the Christian mysteries. As someone once said, there is no injunction against putting old wine into new bottles. And this is what *The Sower* (from its first issue) has been attempting to do. One prays that this 'wine' which we share with our pupils will refresh and inspire them.

ANTHONY F. BULLEN

The background
to religious teaching

Our concern is with teaching religion to the people of *today*. If we are to be effective we need to take note of the theologians who are trying to improve upon the traditional ways of expressing our beliefs, and then make use of their studies in our own presentation of the Christian religion to the various age-groups in our schools. We need to go further. The theologians have been led to re-examine former religious ideas in the light of the evidence arising from the expansion of knowledge in the human and physical sciences. Teachers must be aware of the dominant trends today which influence our understanding of the world and the pattern of life we develop; some of these trends weaken, but can be used to induce, acceptance of Christian faith by young and old.

The outstanding feature in our own life time is the rapid expansion of man's knowledge together with the necessity for individuals to specialize in one particular area. Men have become more critical and exacting in the field of truth and knowledge. It is a welcome development. But one effect of this scholarship is that many have become sceptical of supernatural realities, and they are suspicious of a religion which claims to provide a single comprehensive account of the meaning and purpose of life. 'God made me to know him, love him, etc. . . . .' may have a meaning for believers, but it is alleged to be too naive a statement for the majority of thinking men today.

Adverse factors

The spectacular success of science and technology in recent years has gained for them a universal prestige. But this very prestige has led to a widespread belief that it is to science we must look for all truth. Science either has answers to all our questions or will find them in time. This attitude is found among young people, who tend to reject anything which is not rigorously

1

scientific. They trust the scientist because he is objective and disinterested; they do not trust very much those people who have or seem to have designs upon us — politicians, business men, teachers, yes, even the clergy, who want us to believe all sorts of dogmas that cannot be verified by scientific methods.

Technology makes a bigger impact perhaps than science. By it men have landed on the moon, we can fiddle with our transistor radios and spinwash our underwear, dash away on our scooters. The technologist is the big man today. What is admired about him is that he is essentially a *doer,* one who uses, makes, controls things; he seeks practical solutions to practical problems. Technological culture is ousting traditional culture from the universities and the schools, and it is on the way to ousting faith from the minds of men who now take efficiency and getting tangible results as the norm for judging truth.

It strengthens man in his sense of self-sufficiency; for he is confident that with further research and experimentation he can build an earthly paradise. It tends to make him judge the good life in materialist terms of money, economic comfort and technical gadgets, and be oblivious of ethical considerations.

The knowledge which we now have, thanks to archaeology, palaeontology and the history of comparative religion, of the age of the world and the emergence of man makes incredible to many the Bible teaching of man's origin and destiny; in fact, the whole Bible gives an unacceptable out-of-date world picture, and its only value is that it may give some moral guidance to believers.

The psychologists have investigated the complex layers that go to make up a personality and have made us modify our ideas of freedom and responsibility. Man is indeed free, but he is also unfree, full of numerous determinisms: biological influences, social pressures and his own unconscious past. These factors prevent us from discovering the exact degree of his responsibility, and therefore make it impossible for us to pass moral judgments on human conduct. The anthropologists, for their part, have shown the great variety of customs and practices to be found in different cultures, a fact which seems to rule out the possibility of any absolute ethical standards. Confusion reigns in the field of private and public morality.

The outcome among the young is that they do not know how to think out moral issues or how anyone decides whether anything is good or bad. In saying this I am not subscribing to the alleged breakdown in morals among the young which we often hear and read about. The press and other mass-media present an unbalanced picture of young people's behaviour. The young, it seems to me, are no more immoral than their elders. They are just puzzled; and puzzled chiefly because their parents have not been able or willing to help them. From one point of view, then, we can say that the dominant cultural trends militate heavily against the Christian religion and the teaching of it. But there is a positive side to the picture.

Favourable factors

The sharpened critical sense is leading some people to ask more insistently the basic questions about man and whether science can dismiss the spiritual quality of the universe as an illusion. People are still interested in themselves and their personal relationships. They will study human personality and come to wonder at the mystery of man, and this can lead on to a sense of wonder at the divine which throws light on the mystery.

Science helps considerably to promote human dignity and to create a life worthy of that dignity, since it furthers our understanding of nature and our power over nature. In this twentieth century science, together with technology, has done more than the arts, literature or philosophy to enrich Christian civilization. Science has brought about an enormous improvement in the quality of human life by the way it has served human needs and aspirations. It has done much towards eliminating disease, poverty and suffering from the world — and, we may say, correcting the superstition that these evils are to be passively accepted as the will of God — and the scientists have given us some further idea of the more abundant life which Jesus promises.

It is true that science has often been turned to evil purposes; but this is an abuse which does not nullify its positive work. Nor would the true scientists reject all truths which are not guaranteed by science. They are more modest than their admirers. They believe that consciousness and mental events belong to a different order, and are not to be explained in terms of physics and chemistry. They are aware that reality stretches much further than their field of study.

Through their enthusiasm for technology men might re-examine their idea of God; they will discover that he is not a static Being 'up there', as is commonly imagined, but a dynamic, creative, powerful mystery which surrounds and upholds us in every aspect of life; he is an ever-present personal power which makes and remakes our whole existence as individuals and as a community. In him we live and move and have our being. God is a *doer*. And man, made in the image of this dynamic, creative, controlling God, is meant to share in that character and activity; he is to rule, control and use creation. Man is by nature a doer, a technologist.

The expanded knowledge of the origins of the universe and man should do good in setting man free from the literalist interpretation of the scriptures which still exists among most people. The Bible now has a chance to be seen for what it really is: not a historical book but a religious interpretation of history, a diverse literary heritage, united in its central concerns, but possessing no conscious cohesion, the central concerns being the experiences of a community interpreted as a divine revelation calling for man's response.

Where do we go?

Bearing in mind what the psychologists and anthropologists are saying, we can well understand that young people share their elders' indecision about right and wrong action. They will not accept morality as a clear-cut code handed down by some authority; they see it as something to be painfully worked out by themselves, with guidance, from basic principles. Far from deploring such a situation, the Christian educator should welcome this desire for a personally convinced ethic.

Let us summarize what every sensitive Catholic teacher knows.

1. 'Bible teaching' is doomed to failure. The repetition of the same material through the school years turns the pupils against the Bible in the later secondary years. But even apart from objecting to this boring repetitiveness, the pupils do not under-stand the language and thought-forms of the Bible, and even in the unlikely possibility that they could be brought to some

understanding, the Bible would remain dead because those thought-forms are so very remote from twentieth century western people.

At the same time the teachers rightly hold that the Bible should hold a central place in religious teaching. The question, therefore, is what change should be made in the use of it.

2. Teaching the catechism or any kind of 'straight' religious doctrine is sure to be unsuccessful. Junior children are incapable of it, lower seniors can take a certain amount, upper seniors feel that they are being indoctrinated in the bad sense.

Nevertheless, doctrine is essential. So the question is how best to get across the necessary amount of doctrine for an intelligent convinced living of the faith.

3. Young people are naturally religious. The often maligned teenagers are hungering, perhaps unconsciously, for a religious interpretation of life. They are interested in living. They want to find themselves as persons. They seek meaning to their own lives and that of their fellowmen. They fail to see, through no fault of their own, that religion is so closely interwoven with life as to be indistinguishable. The kind of religious education they have received, concentrating attention on the distant past, has made the Christian religion appear quite irrelevant, negligible in practical life.

The question is how to help them see that in discovering themselves as persons they can come to discover God in whom their deepest needs are met.

The line to take

The conditions of our times and the breakdown of traditional teaching have imposed upon us the necessity to adopt a new approach in religious teaching. Both psychological research and the renewed theology of revelation suggest what the approach should be. We must start from where the pupils are, with their present interests, needs and concerns. The teacher must explore reality together with his pupils, examine real life situations and learn what God may be saying to us today. For God still speaks, as he has always done, in the events of everyday life.

What are the present interests, needs and concerns of young people? Of course, they vary with individuals, but we do know some common elements. Thus one series of questions are of immediate personal importance: those to do with relationships at home, school, and in the neighbourhood; questions connected with a prospective career on leaving school; girl or boy friends, marriage; current events from newspaper articles or television documentaries; incidents raising problems of freedom and responsibility; inner tensions between impulses and desires.

Another set of questions deals with those which every generation puts to itself: what is the origin of the universe? has it a purpose? what is man's place in it? is death the end of everything for him? why be moral?

Young people today are aware of the homeless, the hungry, the refugees, the mentally and physically handicapped. What is being done to remedy this unhappiness? Why all this suffering and pain? They see many different races living in their midst, with different standards of behaviour. Is it possible to judge one race superior to another? If so, how? Why is there racial prejudice?

All these questions have to do with life; they are also basically religious questions, which bears out the view that religion is life. They range over subjects which are not usually associated with religion classes, but touch upon all the subjects in a school curriculum. Now since the theologians are saying that the whole of human existence is the field of God's revelation, educators argue that we ought to be able to devise an integrated school course in which the pupils become aware of the religious aspect in every part of human life.

Religion is not a 'subject'. Our Lord never taught religion; he taught about life and compelled his hearers to examine their lives and find in them a fuller meaning. 'Religious truth', writes Professor M.V.C. Jeffreys, 'is normal experience understood at full depth; what makes truth religious is not that it relates to some abnormal field of thought and feeling, but that it goes to the roots of the experience which it interprets' (*Glaucon — an Enquiry into the Aims of Modern Education*). Religious education then, is not the handing on of a body of Christian truths, but an exploration of experience in depth.

This is the sound principle that underlies the experiments being made in this country to construct an integrated syllabus. So far we have seen nothing published along these lines by Catholics except in *The Sower* (January 1970). A comparison of the suggestions made there with those in, say, the latest agreed syllabuses for the state schools show the greater concern among Catholics for theological content. Catholics seem to be very much aware of the danger of religion being squeezed out by the integrated syllabus or brought in incidentally.

The primary school

In the infant school the teacher knows it is a waste of time to try and teach religious truths, because these children do not understand anything at all unless it comes from their own concrete experience of living. So she aims at multiplying and enriching human experiences upon which a later religious understanding will be formed. Yet even already a certain Christian awareness is being acquired since everything that is good around us bears traces of God's activity. Sister Simon's *Over to You* was the first Catholic book in England to adopt this line.

In the junior school teachers adopt the across-subject thematic approach. The children work upon given themes. They search and discover the depth of their own experiences. The themes, to be truly experimental, must grow out of the children's felt needs at a given age. Here the psychologists come in to suggest suitable themes for the different years. The great name in England for this is Ronald Goldman, though he is not without his critics. The criticisms show what dangers are to be avoided in this life-theme approach: a topic may be presented for far too long with the result that the children become tired of it; a topic, for example light, may be developed in such a way that the children see every interpretation except the religious one; biblical or doctrinal material may be dragged in by the scruff of the neck to make the rest seem religious — and fail. A good example of junior teaching is found in the booklets *Living in God's Family,* edited by P. Wetz and Sister Joyce Mary.

The secondary school

Forms 1 and 2 of the secondary school, ages eleven to thirteen, are nearer to top juniors than to adolescents. These are the best years for religious *instruction,* the imparting of a body of doctrine. But it should be insisted that the instruction be much smaller in content than we have been accustomed to think necessary. All that is needed is a summary statement of the Christian faith, contained in a few pages. It would provide the basic truths and guide-lines to be deepened as the pupils grow up.

In Forms 3 and 4 we adopt a catechesis from life experience proceeding through three stages: sharing experience (personal or vicarious); deepening and widening this experience; seeing the Christian meaning of the experience. In the second stage the teacher will have recourse to a variety of techniques, for example, role-play, drama, play-reading, films, extracts from novels, music, projects, and so on.

In Forms 5 and 6 the young people will be able to engage in more serious discussions. The same life-centred approach will be followed in four stages: a problem is raised through discussion; the problem is analysed in depth; the class discusses the Christian interpretation of the problem; they discuss what it would mean to live out this Christian interpretation in real life today. The reader will find some excellent developments of this method in chapters 11 and 12 of *New Ground in Christian Education* by Harold Loukes.

L. COOKSON

What is at issue in Religious Education today

To be seen truly and in perspective, the problems of religious education today need to be seen in the context of contemporary educational theory and practice. Those of us who have reached middle age can look back to our own schooldays and realize that a very profound change has taken place in the conception of and approach to education since we were at school. This change is not due to the whims of fashion; it is connected with the development that has taken place in the world in which we live, and particularly with the growth of man's mastery over his environment.

Many descriptions are possible of what is meant by an educated man. One of them might be that an educated man is one who is at home in his environment and capable of that kind of response to it which contributes at the same time to his own integrity as a person and to the fashioning of an even better environment for the human race. This is one description among many, but to explore it ever so slightly can give real insight into the contemporary educational process.

To help a man to be at home in his environment means a different thing today from what it would have meant forty years ago. Then it was possible to delimit certain basic skills and a certain sum total of acquired facts which situated a man, made him at home in his world. To function adequately and success-fully in western European culture and to have within oneself the sources of personal growth and social effectiveness one had to be able to read, write and count; one had to have a certain amount of historical and geographical knowledge, an acquaintance with the major works of literature, and if possible some knowl-edge of the works of bygone civilizations which have helped to form our own. These were the elements of basic education that a person needed in order to be at home in western culture. They did not, of course, constitute the whole of education. Character-training, for example, was considered important; and at least at university level there was a different kind of search after truth going on. But the supposition was that in terms of basic education — what we called 'elementary education' — there was a body of knowledge the possession of which constituted the educated man. And it was the function of home and school to supply this knowledge.

The situation is very different today. The boundaries of man's knowledge have widened to an extent that is really amazing. There is no longer a neat body of knowledge, the possession of which makes a man at home in his world. As far as knowledge is concerned a man has to be content to be at home in a small corner of the world, the corner of his specialization. The world has grown too big for any one of us to be at home in the whole of it. Twenty years ago in the U.S.A., the National Register of Scientific and Technical Personnel listed fifty specializations in the field of the natural sciences; so that if you wanted to enter this field and make it your life's work you could choose from among fifty specializations. Today you can choose among nearly a thousand that are now on that same National Register. This is one illustration only of the increased and increasing specialization of knowledge.

So one has, in terms of knowledge, to be content with a small corner, with one specialization. But basic education cannot be concerned with specialized knowledge. In the first place, the choice of a specialization is a mature choice. You have to have some understanding of the whole field before you can choose your specialization. And secondly, in many areas specialized knowledge today develops so quickly that knowledge is out of date almost as soon as it is learned. So basic education no longer aims at giving you specialized knowledge that would so quickly be superseded and useless.

What then does it focus on? It aims at the acquisition of those skills which enable a person to get information and to apply it to new situations. Merely to give a person information is no longer sufficient; he has to know how to find it for himself and (just as important) how to apply it to new situations. Education therefore focuses on the fostering of a spirit of inquiry and research, a spirit that is not disconcerted by the receding of horizons, but is rather stimulated by it. Today we are exhilarated by the sense of infinity we get as the boundaries of knowledge recede. Increasingly we begin to feel that knowledge is not something to possess, but rather something to pursue; and this makes a great difference. Moreover, in education today there is a fostering of integrity in this pursuit, in this research. The value of truth is heightened, as we measure a truth by its degree of conformity not just with statements that have come to us from the past, but rather with the evidence received and with experience. And there is a third area of concern in contemporary education. In this great world where man is at once so small and yet so powerful, where his own possibilities seem to be without limit, the individual can feel terribly lost. An awareness of this gives to education a concern for the strengthening of a sense of personal identity and of significance. Education today is therefore concerned with the working out of a system of values, a struggle towards a perception of meaning. If the world is so great and possibilities so vast, we as men need more than ever to find some meaning to this.

These are the ways in which modern education tries to help contemporary man to be at home in his world. And the fact that they are different from the ways used forty years ago does not mean that our predecessors were stupid, but it means that the world has changed, that man's needs have been modified by the change in his environment, and that he needs to find his whole-ness and contribute to his environment in new ways because of this.

What has all this to do with religious education? We have no sooner asked the question than we find ourselves confronted by a dilemma. Religious education within a believing community is concerned with growth in faith; and faith is our response to God's revelation of himself. On the one hand it is God-given; on the other hand no act is more fully human. Because it is God-given, does it stand so much in a category apart that religious education has nothing to do with education? Or, because no act is more fully human, is our understanding of religious education necessarily influenced by a part of the way we understand education generally?

On this point there is division of opinion among us. There are some who see so clearly and emphasize so strongly the

uniqueness of the experience of faith that it seems to them that
religious education is not to be measured in the categories of
education generally, but must rather be dissociated from it.
They would tend to say that whereas in education generally
there is knowledge to be explored in a spirit of inquiry, with
questioning encouraged and felt as essential to the pursuit of
truth, when it comes to religious education there is a deposit of
definite formulas to be communicated in a spirit of submission
to authority, in a process where questioning leads to doubt and
is therefore to be abhorred. Seen in such an extreme form, this
attitude suggests an unendurable dichotomy within the educational process. On the other hand, there are those who feel that
no such dichotomy can be admitted, that since religious
education is concerned with growing in faith, it is concerned
with growing persons, and therefore must have a close kinship
with general education.

We can go even further. For to those who hold the latter
position it seems possible that the kind of education which this
twentieth century is asking for is perhaps particularly attuned
to the education of faith.

In the March 1971 issue of *Concilium*, Adolph Exeler, a
leading German catechist, wrote: 'When the message of faith
is approached without prejudice, it is seen to have many features
that are identical with education proper.' This is a statement
that is worth testing; and one way of testing it would be to look
again at the characteristics of general education today and see
how well they fit a description of the education of faith.

We saw above that contemporary education is marked by the
unprecedented rate at which the bounds of human knowledge
are receding. There have been other moments in the history of
civilization when the growth of human knowledge has been
accelerated; but never at the rate we see today. And in this there
is perceived a certain quality of infinity; and it is this perception
of the infinity of that which is to be known which makes man a
continual searcher and leads him to see that knowledge is something to be pursued rather than possessed. But if this is true in
the area of intellectual knowledge, it would seem to be supremely
true of the object of faith. In so far as faith is concerned with
some kind of knowledge of God, it must be a continual quest.
We shall surely never cease learning to know him. This knowl-

edge is something that unfolds with life. True knowledge of the living God is not conveyed by books or instruction. But there is certainly this quality of infinity about it. And if in secular knowledge this quality of infinity calls for a spirit of search, should not this be even more true in the realm of faith? Is faith also more concerned with pursuit than with possession?

If this is so, does it not follow that methods of education which foster a spirit of inquiry are eminently proper to religious education? One of the most serious indictments of or allegations sometimes made against Catholic schools is that the system seems to produce people who have no interest in ultimate questions, no inclination to go on seeking, no torment in the face of the problems of life and its deeper meaning. This is a very serious charge. The presentation of a neat code of ideas, a body of belief with the implicit claim to give pre-packaged answers to the problems of life is a poor substitute for the mystery of God. And if it has helped us, to a certain extent, to feel at home in the smaller world of the past, it has always been challenged by personal suffering and tragedy, and is fiercely questioned by the agonizing realities of famine and exploitation and possible self-annihilation which confront us today.

In this line of thought Canon Colomb, in the same issue of *Concilium* writes: 'The new needs of catechesis are clearly to be seen. No longer can it claim to pass on knowledge that is to be acquired once and for all. Like secular education it must rather teach how to learn, train in self-criticism and the need for continual re-statement and revision. Christians need a living faith which is continually developing through grace and the totality of human experience.'

There is a third way in which contemporary secular education and religious education seem very much akin. In the former, knowledge is personalized. Confidence in methods of inquiry comes not so much from the authority of the person who proposes these methods — though this is part of it — but supremely from the things which through these methods I discover. They need not be things which no one has ever discovered before me, but nevertheless I need to discover them for myself. This is important. I do discover them by my own efforts; and the knowledge I have as a result is mine in a particular and peculiar way.

Here too there seems a parallel with faith. My faith is
nothing if not personal. Many people will have mediated this
faith to me; many will have helped it grow. But in the last
instance I cannot live by any man's faith but my own. This does
not mean that a man stands alone in his quest of God, any more
than he stands alone in his quest of learning. In modern education there is much emphasis not only on what we have received
from the past, but also on the value of our present experience
and on our mutual interdependence in the exploration of this
experience. There is a felt need of co-operation, an awareness of
dialogue and discussion as fostering understanding. The relationship patterns are different in this kind of education from the
typical classroom relationship pattern forty years ago. Pupils
are no longer in a learning relationship only with the teacher and
in rivalry among themselves, but now they are in a learning
relationship with each other. And this is paralleled in the area of
faith by our consciousness of the importance of community.

The Christian Church exists as a church by virtue of this.
It is within the religious experience of a people that God reveals
himself to mankind. Jesus himself came at the climax of that
people's history, and as the Christ incorporates into himself a
new people. It is within the religious experience of a people that
each one of us grows in faith, and in solidarity with Christ, with
Christians, with all men, receiving constantly through our
relationship with others both a growth of faith and a deepened
understanding of the faith that is ours.

It seems to me on a relatively superficial observation that the
educational climate of today is in many ways particularly attuned
to such fostering of faith as is the concern of religious education.
I know this is not the whole story. There are aspects of today's
world which test our faith. But in this kind of educational
approach I cannot but see an affinity. This is not to deny the
unique character of faith, which is love as well as knowledge,
which is given as well as received, which implies a commitment
to the person of Christ, which is the greatest and freest act of
the human person. But what that uniqueness implies in educational terms will depend on the way we understand it. If we see
faith as a static thing, given at baptism, sustained by authority,
threatened by inquiry, undermined by doubt, characterized by
clarity, productive of certainty, then we shall feel the modern

world of education very alien to the growth of faith. But if we are committed to a different view of faith, if we see it as a free and personal act fostered by community, growing through ceaseless inquiry, seeming to need tension for its development, working in uncertainty, open to infinity, we shall feel more at home in this educational world even as we shall be driven to examine more deeply still the implications of this for our educational work and the demands it makes upon us.

SISTER RUTH DUCKWORTH

Catechesis
from life experience

It is only natural that there should be development in religious education if educators are taking their work seriously. Whilst general educational practice has made advances in the course of this century we may expect the best ideas to be adopted and adapted sooner or later in religious education. Among Catholics we can distinguish at least three stages through which the process has passed in the last generation or two. Those of us who have reached middle age remember what may be called the catechism phase. At that time the main thrust was to teach people as accurately as possible the truths they must believe, the commandments they must obey and the means of grace they must use. The underlying idea was that revelation is a body of truths which God has committed to his Church; the Church's mission is to transmit these truths to each generation, and these truths are to be found in the councils and in ecclesiastical documents.

New theological insights and progress in educational psychology led to the second stage which came to be known as the kerygmatic approach. Briefly, the idea was that Christianity should be presented as the good news of our salvation in Christ: God lovingly intervenes in human history to draw us to himself and we are to respond in worship and action. The good news is proclaimed in scripture, liturgy, doctrine and in the witness of truly Christian living. Catechesis along these lines became more biblical, liturgical, historical, and proved to be a great improvement upon the previous kind of teaching.

The kerygmatic approach did not, however, produce the hoped for results. Perhaps a main reason for this disappointment was a mistaken view of history, which was taken too much as a record of past events, with the result that teachers dwelt too much upon what God has done for us and not enough on what he is now doing. It was too backward-looking, whereas our pupils live in the present and look to the future. To borrow a phrase of Marshal McLuhan, it could be said: 'We march backwards into the future.' Consequently, today whilst retaining the good elements of the two earlier approaches we have entered upon a third stage of religious education which may be called catechesis from life experience. It is new to priests and parents and to most Catholic teachers, and therefore is easily misunderstood. The new emphases seem to throw into question some traditional assumptions, both theological and educational, and so cause bewilderment and alarm in some quarters.

At the present moment we find in England advocates of the three schools of thought just mentioned. Nothing but harm can result from an out-of-hand condemnation of the new approach without an effort to understand it. Everyone, parent, priest, teacher, wants the best religious education for the children entrusted to his care. Over-hasty rejection of an unfamiliar approach does not contribute to the best interest of those children. What is needed is discussion in a spirit of openness and charity between the holders of different views together with the self-criticism which such discussion will entail so that progress may be made in our common effort: the formation of young Christians into Christ. It is in order to encourage such dialogue that I put down here some elements of a catechesis from life experience.

The theological basis

Catechesis from life-experience is based upon a renewed theology of revelation. 'Revelation', 'God speaks', 'the word of God', all mean the same thing, namely God communicating with men. Being spirit and invisible God reveals himself or speaks or utters his word mediately. He allows a human being to experience his presence and activity in the world so that the person (a prophet in the wide sense) will express them and thereby make him known. Revelation or the word of God, therefore, necessarily implies some human experience, that of the community and of the prophet.

For a long time we used to hold the somewhat static view of revelation as a body of truths made known by God and passed

on from generation to generation as a precious heritage. Now
we take a personalist and dynamic view; we see revelation as
an ever present on-going process in which God speaks to us,
tells us about himself and invites us to friendship. He continues
to do what he has always been doing. He takes men as they are
in their contemporary situations, speaks to them in order to draw
them to himself. It was so in the Old Testament times when
God revealed himself to his people in their contemporary situations. He spoke by deeds and words, closely linked, the deeds
being his saving activity and the words of the prophets being
the explanatory complement of his deeds. It was so in the time
of Jesus to whom God revealed himself as he grew up among
the people of Israel. In fact, the New Testament states that God's
'speaking', this relationship between God and man, reached its
fullness in Jesus Christ. It is so today as God reveals himself
through the still living Christ in the present events of men's
lives.

God speaks to men in various ways which men employ to
communicate with each other, by actions, gestures, signs and
words. He reveals himself in the scriptures; these are a present
word of God to us; for we should see the Bible as an expression of
the Church's constant experience of God. We turn to scripture as
a norm for interpreting the on-going process of revelation. God
also reveals himself in the liturgy, the summit of his continuing
revelation; for here he effects a union with him through the
Spirit of Christ comparable to our own with Christ in the
Eucharist. A further sign of God's revelation are the Church's
dogmas, formulations of the Church's reflections upon the
scriptures and upon her own life under the guidance of the
Holy Spirit. He also speaks through the truly Christian lives
of those men and women who witness to the workableness of
the gospel message.

Far from confining himself to these four signs God reveals
himself in all the things that make up our human existence. He
can and does speak in our work and play, in the sciences and
arts, in literature and technology, and especially in our relations
with other people. God is in this world, living with us, working
with us, inviting us to intimate friendship.

The field of God's revelation is, therefore, human experience,
the experience of men living in community. God takes us as we

are in our contemporary situations and speaks to us in the present events of our lives.

Since all human life can reflect God there is no limit to the ways in which he can choose to speak to men. 'He speaks in the depth and totality of our existence, in the universe as we find it, in the world of technology as we make it, in the history that shapes us, in the future that exerts its exigence upon us, in the present and its possibilities. He speaks in the limitations of our human lives, in our own drives and desires, in our restlessness and frustration, in our experience of loneliness and in the moments of ecstasy of human love and friendship' (M. Hellwig. *Living Light,* Spring, 1969, p. 59).

Of course God's self-revelation is not revelation unless man hears and gives a yes or no response. It is like our speaking to other people. Our speaking invites a reaction of some sort, whether in words or action or perhaps even in silence, as the girl was aware when she said to her teacher: 'We may not seem to be taking it in, but you cannot see what is going on inside.' If man paid no attention whatever to God speaking one could not speak of a revelation. Revelation is a two-way movement, one person speaking and the other hearing. It is important to stress that divine revelation *includes* a yes or no response; man's answer is part of revelation. Without it God is not known and a relationship is not set up. On the other hand, if man responds, at the very least by listening, he is able to grow in knowledge of God.

The special character of *Christian* revelation is that Christ is central to it all. God's word is the expression of God himself, and Christians believe that the word of God became man in Jesus Christ. 'Jesus is man receiving (revelation) as well as God bestowing (revelation)' (G. Moran, *Theology of Revelation,* p. 64). Jesus is truly man; he went through all our basic day by day experiences of relating with others, growing, needing, sharing, choosing and the rest of our human experiences. He is a man who listened to God speaking to him in a first century Jewish community and responded always with love and obedience. The consciousness of his special relationship with the Father dominated his life. After giving a perfect human life-response to God's call, he entered through death upon a new human life, a life transcendently fulfilled. The living Christ, now present in the Christian community, is the one and only mediator of God's revelation. He bestows his spirit to let us share in his own evolving consciousness if only we will listen to him as he speaks through the various media of revelation, namely the events of daily life read in the light of faith by the community of faith; and the community itself receives helps — the scriptures, the liturgy, the magisterium, the life-witness of great Christians — to hear the word of God correctly.

Educational reasons

We have painfully learned that Bible stories and sheer instruction in the facts of religion are no longer effective in leading pupils to think religiously. Pupils are generally apathetic to lessons in which the teachers simply instruct and inform. They are, however, interested in themselves and their own experience. The teacher will be more likely to win their interest and attention if he takes some human experience of theirs, explores it and through it makes them sensitive to some particular aspect of Christian life or belief. He will also help them to become convinced of the personal significance of religion: it has to do with me!

It is a fact of human nature that we experience things first and reflect upon them afterwards. The teacher of doctrine must always take note of this fact. Religious doctrine can, of course, be seen to contain truth in the light of our own Christian experience, but until one has experienced Christianity personally and reflected upon that experience, it means nothing. The crux of the matter is that personal experience must come first. Giving biblical information and catechism answers can do much harm without the priority of experience. Youngsters say, 'What has that to do with life?' That is why we must first arouse in pupils the personal awareness of God's love and power working in the individual's own life, in the world around us and in the whole of human history. It brings the individual into a certain relationship with God and creates in him an attitude of faith and trust.

One often sees quoted nowadays the words of the educationist, Professor M.C.V. Jeffreys: 'Religious truth is *normal experience understood at fullest depth*. What makes truth religious is not that it relates to some abnormal field of thought and feeling but that it goes to the roots of the experience which it interprets' (*Glaucon*, p. 118, my italics). It is inevitable, if we study human beings and their relationship at depth, that we come up against certain questions that impose themselves, ultimate questions about the nature of life and its meaning, which bring us to the ultimate reality that men call God and whom Christians know as Creator and Father. Likewise Mr Harold Loukes, Reader in Education at Oxford University, maintains that almost all the subjects studied in school have basically a religious dimension (*New Ground in Christian Education*). They carry with them certain questions, and these questions are essentially human ones; their profoundest answer must bring in God without whom man cannot be properly understood. And in a Catholic school the teachers will show him to be the God of Christians.

New dimensions in religious education

With this broader conception of revelation we shall transform the old method and content of education into religion. Catechesis becomes the interpretation of human existence in the light of Jesus Christ in order to foster and deepen faith.

For the interpretation of human existence we must know man, the person to whom God speaks, and know him as he really is. He is a very complex being, so that we need to have recourse to the various human sciences and a Christian anthropology.

We need to know him where he is here and now, that is, know the world in which he lives, a rapidly changing world 'at once powerful and weak, capable of the noblest deeds or the foulest. Before it lies the path to freedom or to slavery, to progress or retreat, to brotherhood or hatred' (*The Church in the modern world*, 11). Have we not been too other-worldly in our teaching?

We need to interpret the experience and existence of the students. To interpret is more than to explain. Lots of novelists and philosophers explain naturally and scientifically existing situations, but the 'prophet' discerns and discloses the meaning of events; he reads 'the signs of the times', that is, the trends of contemporary society and the sensibility of contemporary man in so far as they are fraught with religious meaning, and he discloses that meaning to his fellows. And religious educators are prophets of the present human situation.

Experiences are of innumerable kinds. We do well to remember that 'the whole of man's world is expressive of God's revelation in Christ', consequently 'any words, ideas, pictures or experiences which create the possibility of deep personal reflection can have a place in catechetical instruction' (G. Moran *God Still Speaks*). The catechist may, then, look at ordinary events in the life of people in the family, at school, in the neighbourhood, at play, at work, in church, as citizens of a country or of the world, and try to discover what God may be saying here and now to all of us, teachers and pupils; for we know by faith that he is everywhere present in our lives wanting to communicate with us. From among these multifarious events the catechist may like to give preference to the basic human experiences of life and death, love and selfishness, community and alienation, freedom and slavery, creativity and repression, delight and disgust, hope and despair. . . .

Sister Ruth Duckworth reminds us of the important distinction between 'special events' and 'events specially seen'. We have tended in the past to keep exclusively to the former, the Exodus, the exile, the 'Christ-Event', and we tend to expect special events in the Church's life to be used as vehicles of God's communication to man. But surely we ought to be consistent with our convictions of faith. God is at work always and everywhere in his creation. Christian spiritual writers have long been urging us to see God in all things and all things in God. 'Events specially seen' implies seeing the events of daily life in depth, where we discern God's presence and action for and with men in the unfolding of his great loving design.

We interpret human experience in the light of Christ; for he, as we have seen, is the key to everything in the relationship between God and man, the supreme and full revelation of God to us. Jesus Christ who lived a human life has assumed all human realities to himself and gives meaning and value to our human life. In him we discover how to be fully human as God would have us be. In the transformation of the man Jesus, passing from our sinful human condition to a new risen human-divine life God has shown the transformation he intends for every one of us. The 'Christ-Event' (the life, death and glorification of Jesus) is the norm by which we are to look at and interpret our own existence. Catechesis remains Christ-centred whilst being pupil-related.

Foster and deepen faith

The purpose of religious education is to foster and deepen faith. Faith is man's answer to God's revelation in Christ. As the divine self-revelation is complex and inclusive, so also is the personal answer which is faith. It includes first of all a full personal surrender to the person of Christ, staking one's whole life in reliance on him. Christ is God for us. This commitment means a readiness to make sacrifices of one's own pet ideas in order to live the new life which Christ proclaims, promises and bestows on his followers. Psychologically, the most outstanding feature of the commitment of faith is trust: a man gives his full allegiance to Christ and is willing to face the unknown with complete confidence in him; he is willing to enter on a whole new way of living, the life of faith. Besides commitment, faith includes acceptance of Christ's message. A man gives an assent of the mind to the truth of the Christian message. Although some of the content of the teaching may be difficult to accept, he believes Christ's teaching because he believes in Christ himself.

Demands upon the teacher

Teaching from life-experience makes great demands upon the teacher; it calls for versatility and sensitiveness. With younger children one can take something they can see, for example a desk, and discuss it until they reach a conclusion that God and man together made the desk, and so there is a relationship between God and man. But with more mature teenagers it will require great sensitivity to discern with them what God might be saying through events and happenings in their own lives or that of society as a whole.

The teacher needs to be possessed of a sound theology which makes him aware that authentic human values have been transformed and made more real through Christ who is at present working in men's lives. He will see Christ behind any manifestation of love and service among people and he will help his pupils to discover Christ in a discerning acceptance of human values. Here lies one main difference between the Christian and the good secular humanist; the former takes a wider perspective of human nature than the latter, who sees human life entirely within a framework supplied by the concepts of the natural sciences.

More thought must be given to the process of communication. Marshal McLuhan has made us realize that the mass media are changing us whilst informing us, and that they are nowadays not just helpful but a necessary condition for human development. Theology tells us that God can convey his message through the forms of contemporary art, scientific technology and literature. Part of the teacher's task will be to find and use those media which speak best to the students and by means of them coach the students to think as Christians and ask the right questions. He looks for Christ in the midst of human experience, of life as it is actually lived, in the exercise of liturgy and in our daily behaviour, in the gospel as it has been written and above all in the way in which it is lived today.

W. HEALEY

A new approach
to Religious Education

The gap between pundit and practitioner

Teachers of religious education are as aware as any other educationist of the problems posed by the generation gap and the credibility gap, both of which bedevil the relationships at all levels between teacher and taught. There is a third kind of gap, the existence of which is not always openly acknowledged. Specialists in the educational field, whether they be inspectors or training college lecturers, always seem to come up with something new just when the poor teacher is beginning to think he is about to master the old. The result is a gap, a chasm rather, between the two which often leads to confusion or despair on the teacher's part.

There is certainly much confusion and not a little despair among religious education teachers. They watched the catechetical movement, largely the work of 'experts', struggle through methodology into content, from the 'how' to the 'what'. Courses and programmes, the 'when', came next, and many thought that all their problems were being solved. Disillusionment, however, is growing; for with the appearance of the new syllabuses has come a realization that the 'experts' who were ultimately responsible for the new programmes are the very people who are now repudiating them. There is, in fact, an ever-widening catechetical gap between pundit and practitioner.

In the secondary school many teachers are still using Fr F. Somerville's pre-Council series; others have adopted Fr D. Konstant's syllabus or *Over to You* or *Eleven to Sixteen* or *Young Christians Today*, though this last is basically a rendering of the oldest of the new courses, published as far back as 1950 by Belgian Jesuits. Others who are still looking for a good syllabus are usually disappointed when they ask somebody knowledgeable about the best book to adopt. It seems as if the leaders in catechetics are not keen on any syllabus at all. No name is more respected at the moment among English and American experts than that of Gabriel Moran, and he is on record as maintaining: 'Contrary to what is often said today, our chief need is not detailed programmes and more practical applications for religion teachers. We ought to stop attempting to create these "*a priori*", because we always end up with the pseudo-concrete, the pseudo-practical, new frustrations and more disappointments' (*God Still Speaks*, p. 24). No wonder the ordinary teacher is confused.

The argument against a syllabus in religion

What exactly is it that catechists object to in the new syllabuses? In many cases it is the linear structure: first year, salvation history; second year, sacraments; third year, morality; fourth year, Church. Some courses, such as the Westminster syllabus, stick to this plan but avoid a rigid and exclusive application of it. Others, like D. Lance's *Eleven to Sixteen* repudiate it altogether. But these have their own linearity, and it is difficult to see how it can be avoided if one is going to plan at all.

Yet Brother Moran would object to each of them on the grounds that 'it is still a *system,* a rigid construction of words and ideas imposed upon people from the outside to manipulate their lives'. He maintains that such 'a blunt, frontal attack upon a person's freedom with a mass of religious concepts and practices is bound by the nature of the case to fail' (*God Still Speaks*, pp. 43, 44). Followers of Brother Moran find a contradiction in the phrase 'religion syllabus'. A syllabus implies a fairly formal and rigid structure imposed on the class, whereas religion ought to respect the principal issue in the world today, which is the freedom of the individual. We ought in fact to start, not with a body of religious material, which we then organize to suit the consecutive years of the pupils' school career, but with the pupils themselves, their interests and aspirations at the particular stage in which we find them. God reveals himself to them precisely in this daily activity and especially in the inter-personal relationships it involves, and the catechist's task is so to clarify and deepen everyday experience that God's revelation can shine through. This does not eliminate the biblical word, the liturgical action, the ecclesiastical decision, but it does not start from them, it does not structure the whole course on them. God's Word is spoken in the child's relationships within his own world, and so it is that world which must form the raw material out of which the programme is constructed.

A bit of realism

The ideal way to fulfil such a programme is obviously to integrate religious education with other subjects, especially the humanities. A sincere open enquiry into any topic of modern interest, for example authority, friendship, war, freedom and so on, undertaken by a group which is at least nominally Catholic, must bring the students face to face with the ultimate realities of life as they affect their particular age-group, must lead them to Christ and his Church.

But let us be practical. There are at the moment very few secondary schools, Catholic or otherwise, conducting courses which are genuinely integrated, though there are many R.O.S.L.A. schemes on paper which may eventually alter this situation. What we have in practice are subject-directed syllabuses which include a few periods of 'R.E.' each week during which the catechist has to work in isolation from the other subjects.

Real situations demand practical solutions. There are still thousands of religion teachers in Catholic schools who need guidance and help — and need it now. It is unrealistic to tell the average teacher that he ought not to adopt any of the syllabuses on the market, but should work out his own, relying on his own experience of where his children are at any particular stage of development. He has to have a programme. I would suggest that he be encouraged to keep it flexible, to experiment with it, to concentrate on particular themes, to consult other syllabuses for ideas and methods. But he still needs some guidance as to what and when, if not how.

In fact, most Catholic teachers are very unhappy if they are not given a set of text-books. And yet many of us are convinced, with Brother Moran, that to plump for any of the current fixed programme text-books is to slam the door on all that we have come to consider desirable in modern catechetics — openness, flexibility, relevance, topicality. The only practical solution is a compromise. In the present state of affairs, the best way out would seem to be short, flexible programmes, continuously reconsidered and re-written, supplemented by carefully chosen excerpts from what is available in the way of text-books and by practical guidance in how to apply them.

Presuppositions

Later on I shall quote one year from my own five-year programme and indicate how these ideas are applied in it; but before going into detail it might be profitable to outline the attitude on the part of the teacher which is considered a necessary prerequisite before any such programme can be made to work.

1. First, the teacher should attempt to get the pupils used to *working in groups*. You may say that group work — especially in connection with theme development — is now so common in the primary school that one can take it for granted that the children are already experienced at it. Whether this is strictly true or not, there are primary schools which work an integrated syllabus, based on themes, but specifically exclude religious education from the general programme! In any case, group work is very far from being an established feature in most secondary schools.

The important point about this group work is that the pupils become accustomed to helping one another, especially in finding out and understanding things. It means doing away with encouraging them to rivalry, by offering prizes for the best work. They can still be rewarded, but not for surpassing others. Mutual co-operation and help are the important factors in religious education.

2. Second, we must get them used to *activity*. The religion class, if it is distinguished at all from the others, is the one where they *do* something. Not a place where they are told what to do, how to do it and what the results are to be: we want a genuine spirit of investigation, of finding out, of judging and estimating.

That is why the first form themes in my case are set out in the form of work-sheets or work-programmes, prepared by the teacher, to be given out to the pupils. These can work each at his or her own individual pace and the teacher may then be able to talk to individuals and discuss problems at a more personal level. Every now and then, usually in response to an appeal from the pupils, the teacher can indicate lines of approach and interpretation and apply the material to current topics of interest. Nobody need fear that with the handing out of a work-sheet the job of the teacher will be ended: he will have to work harder than ever under this method (the work-sheet system is still suitable for Form 2, but in older forms will be less acceptable).

3. The aim of the religion lesson is not to make the pupil learn a body of knowledge which, he is informed, has never changed in the past and which, he is assured, will never alter in the future. On the contrary, he ought to become more and more aware in the course of his classes that the religious life, the life of God, is infinitely adaptive, is constantly growing and developing, both for the individual and for the whole Church.

4. We should try to give pupils some understanding of the *Christian community* as the people who continue the work of Christ in the world. Two corollaries of this proposition can at least be touched on. First of all, there are people who are doing Christ's work, that is, creating a loving community and so a presence of Christ, under the guidance of his own Spirit — but not consciously or specifically, those, for example, who feed the hungry, but say they do not know Christ. Secondly, this work of Christ's will take a special form in different areas and at different epochs.

5. Apart from their experience of the Christian community, we should try to give the children some knowledge of the *personality of Jesus*. The stories with which we make them familiar will stress his general friendliness and his concern for others, especially the outcasts of society. There will be no emphasis on the miraculous.

6. They should gain some experience of *community worship*. The content of that worship, whether it involves Mass, assembly or class services, should be firmly based on their own life experiences and their work as a class group. Further, they should take for granted that they themselves should help in composing the available sections of this worship: what is said and done

should really be said and done by them, in their own words and actions.

7. As far as sin and repentance affects them we should try to train them to *see their own faults and failings in the context of the community* or communities to which they belong. We should try to avoid laying stress on sin as the individual's failing to observe a fixed code of morality.

8. Throughout the course we should encourage them by word and example to *pray spontaneously,* both in their own private prayers and in class worship. The subject of their prayers would naturally be their own activities, including those worked out in these classes, and other contemporary happenings.

Example

The scheme I myself use is based on a number of themes which I consider relevant for the particular age-group in question. Here is a brief outline of the first four years:

1. a) Who I Am (Incarnation)
   b) What I Do (Eucharist)

2. a) Leadership
   b) Change
   c) Helping people

3. a) Becoming a person
   b) Getting in touch with others
   c) Other persons

4. a) Relationships
   b) Choices

Let me take the second year as a particular example. For this class the following points have to be kept in mind:

1. The questions are addressed to the pupils in the form given here, that is, they look like condensed work-sheets. However, the teacher may prefer to take each item as it comes, without handing the whole term's work to the pupils. Whatever method is adopted, we should allow the pupils to work at different speeds and at different depths. The work must be truly

personal, whether it is done individually or in groups, and this is particularly important with mixed ability classes.

2. The particular classes I have in mind were already equipped with *New Outlook Scripture*, Book 2 (The Old Testament). In addition I have made copies of Alan Dale's *New World* available for class use only. Both of these have been utilized in this syllabus to help teachers who like text-book work.

3. Even if work-sheets are given, the teacher must still be very active in the programme. The pupils will not be able to tackle some of the questions without his help and thus he will often have to give lessons to groups or to the whole class. All the time he must be alert in helping individuals who need information or encouragement.

4. Some teachers tend to panic when their pupils remain overlong at the secular aspects of the theme. But they must resist the temptation to pull the class away from what is interesting them on the plea that they have to get on with religion. Only if the theme is thoroughly explored — at the twelve to thirteen year old level, of course, — will the pupils really feel the relevance and importance of the religious aspect when they come to it in the natural course of events.

5. Furthermore, if the teacher feels that the groundwork for an understanding of the Incarnation and the Eucharist (year 1) has not been adequately laid, then of course he must do some remedial work on these, as the occasion offers.

6. The second year programme should itself go some way towards counteracting the rigid impersonal attitude to morality of the average second former, and the teacher will need to be continually alert to every opportunity offered by the scheme of developing in his pupils a genuine personal code of conduct.

SECOND YEAR

1st term — LEADERSHIP

1) Study photographs of some famous leaders, e.g. J. F. Kennedy, Martin Luther King, Gandhi, the Queen, Prince Philip, Fr Gauthier, Fr Borrelli, Sue Ryder, Football/Hockey Captain. . . .

2) Choose any two from these or other leaders you know and write a biography of them with illustrations.

3) Can you answer the following questions about the leaders you chose?
   (a) What made them good leaders?
   (b) What did they expect their followers to do?
   (c) What difficulties did they experience in getting their followers to do this?
   (d) What resemblance did you notice among the leaders themselves?

4) Make a list of great leaders, past and present. Now arrange these in columns according to the work they did.

5) From your text-book study the following leaders of God's people: Moses, the Judges, Samuel, Saul, David, Solomon. Apply the questions in 3 to each of them.

6) Write an illustrated biography of Jesus.

7) In what way was he like the other leaders you have written about?

8) Write down the names of Jesus' twelve special followers.

9) Find out as much as you can about how he picked each of these to be his special friend. (E.g. in *New World*, pp. 10, 139.)

10) Act or mime one or more of these stories.

11) Jesus' work was to tell everybody this good news:
   (a) God is our Father and loves us, whether we are good or bad;
   (b) we ourselves ought to love everybody, friends and enemies.

   He also gave us the power to follow what he taught.

   The parables of the prodigal son and of the good samaritan illustrate (a) and (b). Retell them in a modern way and draw a picture for each of them.

   Tell or illustrate some miracle stories from the life of Jesus which show God's power and love.

12) The apostles did not always find it easy to follow the teaching of Jesus. Read these passages from the Bible,

choose the two you like best and copy them out. Draw a picture to illustrate one of them.

'They came into a village in Samaria, but the people would not have anything to do with them because they were Jews. Seeing this, the disciples James and John said, "Lord, do you want us to ask God to send down fire to burn them up?" But Jesus told the two disciples off and they just went on to another village' (Lk 9).

'The disciples came to Jesus and said, "Who is going to be the greatest in your kingdom?" So he called a little child to him and put the child in front of them. "I am telling you", he said, "unless you change and become like little children, you'll never even get into my kingdom" ' (Mt 18).

'Peter came up to him and said, "Lord, how often have I got to forgive my brother when he does something wrong to me? As much as seven times?" Jesus' answer was, "Not seven times, I tell you, but seventy times seven times" ' (Mt 18).

'People were bringing little children to Jesus so that he could touch them and say a prayer for them. The disciples wouldn't let them do it. So Jesus said to his followers, "Leave the children alone. Don't stop them coming to me. These are the kind I want for my kingdom" ' (Mt 19).

'The soldiers rushed forward, grabbed Jesus and arrested him. Then one of his followers pulled out his sword and aimed a blow at one of the Temple soldiers, cutting off his ear. Jesus said, "Put back your sword. Those who use weapons will themselves be killed by them" ' (Mt 26).

13) When Jesus was born there were different people trying to be leaders in Palestine: the Romans, the kings, the Sadducees, the Pharisees, the Essenes, the Zealots. Find out about them from Chapter 9 of your book.

Read the two accounts of the Birth of Jesus. See if you can find out from these what kind of leader Jesus was going to be. How was he going to be different from the six above?

2nd term — CHANGE

1) Do a project on changes that have taken place in the world, e.g. in transport, clothing, farming, houses, schools. . . . Different groups could choose different topics and combine their results at the end.

2) Study Chapters 6, 7, 8 of *New Outlook Scripture*, Book 2. Notice how most of the changes seemed great evils at the time: bad kings; foreign invasions; loss of freedom, kingdom, capital city, temple. They had to change their ideas as a result.

3) Think back over your own life and note the changes that have taken place in yourself: in growth, abilities, friends, house, school, hobbies. Write about these changes and illustrate them if you can.

4) Read the story of one of these people and tell in your own words about the big change that took place in his or her life: Ignatius Loyola, Douglas Bader, Christy Brown, Sally Trench.

5) In the life of Jesus the biggest change we are told about was the starting of his public life. How many things did he have to change at that time?

6) Find out, by reading or asking questions, what changes were made in their lives by Peter, Matthew, Judas, after Jesus asked them to follow him.

7) Make a list of the faults that prevent children of your age becoming good followers of Jesus.

8) Look back to what you wrote in no. 11 of last term. Why did the prodigal son change? What are we told about in the story that did not change before or after?

9) Lent is the time of year when Catholics all together make an effort to change their lives and to become better followers of Jesus. Make a list of changes that you think people of your age should make at this time. (They should include both things to stop doing and things to start doing.)

10) Make a coloured chart showing how Lent fits into the whole Church's year.

11) At the beginning of Lent Catholics put ashes on their heads.
Find out: (a) how this custom started; (b) what it means to us today.

12) What sacrament of the Church will be of great help to us if we want to pass Lent well? Explain why.

13) Lent is a preparation for Easter and Easter has always been connected with the sacrament of baptism. Write an account of the baptism ceremony from the Easter Vigil, with illustrations.

3rd term — HELPING PEOPLE

I — LOVE CAN DO ALL THINGS
Study the story of Helen Keller or Leonard Cheshire to illustrate this. Try to prepare a T.V. programme from one of the stories.

II — CHRIST'S LOVE IN ACTION TODAY
Study the way Jesus helped others and how he continues this work today through people. In each case the story of what Jesus did could be read and discussed with the rest of the class, and then the corresponding present-day work could be studied, for example through newspapers and magazines. Perhaps also you might be able to meet people from hospitals, homes or missions. You could then work in groups and build up a large class collage to illustrate what you learned.

JESUS' CONCERN FOR PEOPLE	HIS SPIRIT WORKING TODAY
1) *The Sick* Simon's mother-in-law, etc.	Visiting the sick
	Hospital work
The blind	Work for blind, deaf, dumb
The lame	Helping the handicapped
The deaf and dumb	

2) *The Poor* Becoming poor   Charitable works
                    himself   Shelter
   The Beatitudes   Crusade of Rescue
   The rich young man   UNESCO, Oxfam, etc.
   The widow's mite

3) *The Sad* Widow of Naim   Sympathy for others in need
   Jairus   Mother Teresa
   Martha and Mary   Father Pire
   The Women at Calvary   Leonard Cheshire

4) *The Outcast* Lepers   The Simon Community
   Demoniacs   The Samaritans
   Mary Magdalen   Sally Trench
   The Samaritan Woman   The Human Rights
   Zaccheus   Movement

III — WORK OF THE SPIRIT

1) Look back to the first term's work on leadership, no. 12, and go over again the stories of the apostles. Now read about their behaviour after the resurrection. (Dale, Bk 3, Pt 2, *Across the World.*)

2) Compare in detail the behaviour of Peter before and after the resurrection. Why was he able to overcome the weakness he showed at the crucifixion.

3) We too can overcome our faults by the help of the Spirit of Jesus. Make up a story or a play in which this happens to you. Or you can write a poem or a song about it.

4) Read St Paul's account of his experience of the resurrection of Jesus (Dale, Bk 4). And write down what he learned on the road to Damascus about the Christian community.

5) Our Christian community today meets for Mass. What then does St Paul's experience tell us about that meeting? Refer back to Form 1, B — 'What I Do', Sheet 1, 'Meetings'. Try to illustrate it by a diagram or collage.

J. CLARK

Faith and articles of faith

Many adults in England once became Catholics because they wanted a stable Church, one which would state authoritatively what God has revealed. Today they are deeply disturbed, because now there seems to be no certainty and no unity of teaching. Can anything be done to help them? Did they make a mistake in the first place by seeking an illusory security?

If a man wants to become a Roman Catholic he is told that he must accept all that the Church teaches. But is all of her teaching credible? for example, 'Outside the Church . . .' and the bodily assumption of Mary as these have been commonly understood, and some of the Church's moral principles? And suppose he becomes a Catholic, can he bring himself to affirm each and every dogma with personal conviction? Can a Grimsby fisherman be held to profess with personal conviction that the only-begotten Son is one in substance with the Father; or must a university don give up intellectual integrity if he cannot see any meaning or point in affirming that Adam and Eve were a single couple or the Father and the Son are not two principles but one co-principle of the Holy Spirit?

Ask any ordinary Catholic what he believes and he will probably answer you in the words of the Apostles' Creed or of the catechism. Ask him to say in his own words what he really believes and he will probably be reluctant to speak, for fear of appearing technically a heretic. It is a sign that he is unsure of himself. Many Catholics have doubts and questions which they repress, and they use official formulas, such as catechism answers, as an escape way of saying what they believe. Is it healthy that there should be such a division between personal belief and official statement? Can we speak of a free personal response of faith in such an individual?

Intelligent young Catholics in our schools and universities are feeling the crisis of faith perhaps more acutely than most of us; they are saying: 'I cannot take the Church's teaching. It is unreal. It seems to have nothing to do with this world of

science and technology. It assumes a general world-view which
is quite obsolete.' Are they losing or rejecting faith?

Many adult Catholics are like the anguished writer in the
Universe recently who is completely bewildered by the controversies going on in the Catholic press and wonders whether there
is any unity of faith nowadays. In their sadness, however, they
cling to prayer and the sacraments. Can anything be done to
enlighten or strengthen them?

What about ourselves? We are schizophrenics. We preserve
the mediaeval idea of an opposition between the world and the
Church. The Church is the ark of salvation. The world is one
of the enemies of the soul. The good Christian stands aloof from
it. At the same time we feel we are very much in this wonderful
secular world and would not like to be out of it for five minutes.
We have values which come from the old mentality and values
from the secular world. Hence there is a tension in us. Shall
we retreat to the haven of the protective Church and be saints,
or go into the secular world and be human?

These are only a few of the situations we meet with regarding
faith today. We shall never be without difficulties and problems
in some form or another because faith is acceptance of and
committal to what we cannot see, and therefore it is constantly
producing crises and tensions. But each generation has to cope
with them and make the life of faith liveable.

The basic reason, I am convinced, why we have most of our
present difficulties is that Catholics have been brought up on
an incomplete view of faith. The catechism answer to the
question 'What is faith?' illustrates my point. Faith, it is
said, is believing without doubting whatever God has revealed.
It is an assent of the mind to truths which we cannot understand,
but which we accept on God's authority. Another common way
of putting it is to say that faith is acceptance of what the Church
teaches inasmuch as the Church is the mouthpiece of God.
Catholics have adopted a strongly intellectualist view of faith as
an assent to propositions, called dogmas or articles of faith. They
have inherited a view that came into prominence as a result of
Counter-Reformation controversies.

The Second Vatican Council has moved us away from this
inadequate view of faith and recovered for us the biblical under-

standing of it. It puts before us *full faith*. If we follow its lead,
I am convinced we shall overcome many of our difficulties and
help our pupils to grow in a personal living faith.

What faith is

Let me outline very briefly what faith is. Faith is *primarily
a personal relationship*. It is the acceptance of a personal relationship with a personal God who reveals himself to men and
invites them to friendship.

Revelation and faith go together inseparably. For faith is the
correlative of God's revealing himself to men. The two of them
constitute the one mystery of God's encounter with man.

In establishing this relationship God makes the first move.
He comes and speaks to man in a variety of ways, but most
clearly and fully in Jesus Christ, the Word of God become man.
At the same time he calls man from within, through what we
call the workings of the Holy Spirit, who opens men's minds
and hearts to enable them freely to accept the offer of friendship.

God not only makes the initial move, he also sustains a
man in his steps to full mature faith. This is why Our Lord
could say 'No one can come to me unless the Father draws
him' (Jn 6. 44), and why the Church teaches that faith is a gift
of God.

Now look at man's side. When God speaks a man might
refuse to listen or he might reject the call. If, however, he does
listen to the word of God and accepts the invitation to live in
union with him, he makes the response of faith. This human
response is not so much an act or a series of acts, as rather a
basic all-embracing attitude of mind and heart which gives a
new direction to the whole of a man's life. Christian faith is
a comprehensive Yes to God revealing himself in Christ. A
personal relationship has been set up.

This personalist understanding of faith is what needs to be
placed first and urgently stressed, because it has long been
neglected and the neglect has given rise to misunderstandings
of our religion.

A personal relationship, as anyone knows from human
experience, is a complex reality. It has many elements and can
be looked at from various angles. As it would take too long to

analyse the faith relationship here, I will confine myself simply to listing one or two features which are of immediate relevance to this essay.

Faith is the response of the *whole* person — his mind, will and all his activity — to God who gives himself in Christ. Since the encounter between God and man takes place in Christ, we Christians say that faith is a commitment of the whole person to the person of Christ, as whole-hearted as that of the apostles when they shared a fellowship of life with him before the resurrection, and after it surrendered themselves to him with absolute confidence and love.

I stress this close personal adherence to Christ the Saviour because we must be convinced that faith is not in the first place an assent to dogmas, as we have been led to think. It is a person-to-person surrender.

Psychologically speaking, the most outstanding feature of faith is *trust*. Suppose one of you tells me you are a teacher. I will believe what you say. But before I can say: 'I believe what you say', I must be able to say: 'I believe *you*, you who tell me this about yourself'. Likewise, before I can say: 'Lord, I believe what you tell me about yourself' I must be able to say: 'I believe *you*; I put my trust in you. My experience arising from contact with you convinces me of your believableness'.

Thus the primary datum of faith is not a statement of any kind, but a person whom I trust. I draw attention to this point because old controversies caused Catholic theologians to let this trust character of faith to drop into the background in their anxiety to emphasize the necessity of works and the assent to propositions.

Faith is a *life-long* activity. We cannot say that faith is acquired once and for all by a single decision to opt for Christ. It is a personal relationship that needs to be cultivated in all the changing circumstances of life. Faith may be compared to the love between husband and wife which deepens, develops and matures as they share life together with its ups and downs. Their love endures through times of trial and need. Similarly, the surrender of faith is life-long, with its ups and downs in changing situations; the faith-relationship with Christ can weaken and even collapse unless it is constantly strengthened through attention, prayer and struggle for greater solidity.

Finally, Christian faith is not a private affair between the individual and God. It is something we possess in common. It is a community experience. Christian faith is possible only within the community of believers. Think of your own faith, whether you are a cradle Catholic or an adult convert from unbelief. Its birth and later growth occurred through the medium of particular personal and social influences. That medium was and remains the community of believers whom God had already called together, which we call the Church. God speaks to men in and through the Church, Christ's Body. This community is, as a matter of fact, the immediate recipient of revelation. It is the *locus* for the birth and growth of Christian faith. In the concrete, for the birth of faith the occasion may have been the accident of being born into a Christian family, or the example of a Christian acquaintance, or a preacher addressing a crowd; through them it is the Church bearing witness. For growth in faith we may feel indebted to parents, a school, a parish, or a group of committed Christians; but these are as it were cells of the total Church community.

Thus faith has an ecclesial character; my commitment is to Christ living in the community where I meet him, a fact which has implications for the individual who is expected to believe what the community believes and not branch off into sectarianism.

Faith as knowledge

So far I have spoken of faith as a personal relationship, the aspect which needs to be put first and kept first in our thinking and teaching. We come now to the other main aspect.

God, speaking to us in Christ, tells us about himself, about ourselves and what he intends for us. There is a communication of knowledge. As it is a communication from one person to others, we call it a message, the Christian message. It also goes by other names: the gospel, the content of revelation, the deposit of faith.

The point to be noted now is that *faith implies knowledge*. This knowledge derives from the relation set up by the commitment we make. We listen to what Christ says and we accept his message. So full faith means that we *consent* to live the life of

D

friendship with him (faith as commitment) and we *assent* to what he makes known (faith as knowledge). The assent is essential to faith, even though it is derivative and secondary.

The content of revelation is really very slight. It can all be summed up in one sentence: the content of revelation is 'the good news is that God offers life in Christ to all men even though they have done nothing to deserve it' or if you prefer another one: 'Christ our saviour has come to bring us life and to give it to us more abundantly'. That is the essential core of the gospel message as made known to us in the writings of the New Testament.

However, it is both natural and necessary that we try to understand as best we can the gospel message, and express it in creeds and precise statements according to the needs of various generations.

It is natural to do so, because it is perfectly normal for all of us to want to grow in knowledge of someone we love and to whom we have dedicated our lives. Inevitably, we, that is, the believing community, formulate for ourselves what Jesus has told us about himself and his Father and the demands his friendship makes upon our style of life.

More important, the experience of the Church from the beginning has shown the necessity of expressing its faith in special formulas. In the days of the apostles the leaders were obliged to do this for purposes of catechesis, liturgy and the struggle against heresies which had already begun to sprout. Within the New Testament writings we find traces of the primitive communities articulating their faith in the form of *creeds* (see Mt 29.19; Eph. 4.4-6; Phil. 2.6-12; Tim. 2.5). It suggests what we easily acknowledge, namely that you cannot have faith as commitment without explicit verbal statements of what you believe. The Church gives objective precision to the content of faith.

The early generations of Christians seem to have got along with few if any statements of that precise and authoritative kind which we call *dogmas*. A dogma is a statement of something contained in divine revelation and formulated by the teaching authority of the Church, or better, by the whole body of the Church. Dogma is rooted in scripture; it is of a piece with God's scriptural word, which it clarifies. It is an article of faith, which a Christian must believe, for example, 'the Son of God is begotten not made'.

Since the fourth century dogmatic pronouncements have increased in number to a very considerable extent. Some people like this multiplicity: Fr Faber said he would like to see a new dogma from Rome every morning when he opened *The Times*. Others do not like it: they say this multiplicity of dogmas can make us lose sight of the unity of the faith.

Dogmas

Because Catholics have made the mistake of putting the emphasis on the secondary aspect of faith, a habit which has landed us in difficulties today, let us consider a few things about these dogmas.

Dogmatic formulas are always inadequate

Dogmas say something true about the faith, but they are incapable of fully translating the mysterious reality they point to. The object of faith is a person, Jesus Christ. The Church's knowledge of him arises from an *experience* of him. Our dogmatic formulas are an effort to verbalize this living experience. Yet we know from our ordinary human experience that no matter how well we know a person and no matter how fully he discloses himself, there is always a certain centre of the self which remains incommunicable and inviolable; there is always some area which cannot be fathomed. Still more is this true of Jesus Christ, the God-man. No matter how much he tells us of himself and his Father, there is always much which eludes our understanding. We are right to try and penetrate more deeply his self-communication, but our success is always partial, our knowledge is always imperfect. Consequently, our dogmas are always imperfect, inadequate.

Dogmas need to be reformulated

The Church, whose task is to propose revelation and expound it anew in each age of history, must rethink and reformulate its dogmas. We cannot simply go on repeating what was said by previous generations. I am afraid that too many pastors are 'repeaters' and not re-thinkers. They take the view that revelation reached its completion with the death of the last apostle and that we have nothing more to do than repeat what was then good news. But against this view we need to remember that everything that is expressed in human words — whether it be scripture, creeds or dogmas — is time-conditioned by language and cultural context.

Language may be our most precise and reliable way of communicating, but it has its limitations. The meaning of words changes in the course of time. Readers of *The Canterbury Tales* soon discover that many English words had a very different significance in Chaucer's day from what they have now. And the same alteration of language exists with regard to ancient dogmatic formulas. A classic example is that of 'nature' and 'person' as used by Chalcedon with reference to Christ. The words had a particular meaning for the people of those days which is quite different from what they mean to twentieth century Europeans.

This question of language has become serious for us today. By clinging to traditional formulas in her official teaching the Church has formed a private religious language which is intelligible only to well-educated believers. It is unintelligible to people with no religious background, yet to whom the gospel must be preached. It is confusing to the majority of Catholics because they are expected to integrate two languages and two ways of thinking, the traditional language of Church documents and their ordinary language of contemporary life. Surely, if we want the faithful to understand properly the articles of faith, we need to revise the antiquated expression of much of our teaching.

Dogmas are time-conditioned by their cultural context, and therefore need to be re-interpreted for their true meaning to come home to men of today. Most of our dogmas took shape in the patristic and mediaeval periods. The thought patterns of the fathers and of the mediaeval theologians were quite different from ours. They thought in pre-scientific categories. For centuries the Church has been expressing its doctrines within a Thomist system of philosophy, whereas today only a very few people are acquainted with Thomism, and even among Catholics a personalistic philosophy is beginning to predominate. For centuries everyone held a rather static view of man and the universe, whereas today with the expansion of knowledge we take a dynamic evolutionary view of reality. It was no doubt because of these immense cultural changes that Pope John called upon the Second Vatican Council to restate the faith in 'the literary forms of modern thought', and the Council has implicitly committed the Church to reinterpreting its dogmatic heritage in such a way that the gospel message will stand out clearly in the new contemporary self-understanding.

A right understanding of *tradition* requires that we re-think and re-formulate the ancient articles of faith. I say a right understanding because ever since the Council of Trent most Catholics have thought of tradition as a 'source' which contains revelation alongside scripture, a source from which one can draw dogmas. It is a much too static concept of tradition which cannot do justice to the fullness of this living phenomenon.

More recently, that is, since the nineteenth century, a deplorable restriction of tradition to the official teaching of the magisterium has been in fashion. The dominant theologians of the Roman school before and during the First Vatican Council gave the impression that the Church is primarily a hierarchical institution which exists to save people. The most important persons in it are the pope and the bishops, because they alone have the special power from Christ to teach, rule and sanctify. Tradition was defined by one of them (Perrone) as 'the living, authoritative preaching of the word of God by the hierarchy'. The same tendency continued during the first half of this twentieth century as theologians stressed the work of the magisterium and the popes themselves got into the habit of writing encyclicals and issuing papal decrees. And to make matters worse still, as the official teaching of the magisterium can be gathered together in documents, tradition was thought of as something that could be enclosed within a source book, such as Denzinger's *Enchiridion Symbolorum*.

It has taken the Second Vatican Council and the ecumenical dialogue of our own days to do away with this restricted view. Tradition is now seen as the activity of the old whole Christian community. It is the common life of the Church with 'all that she herself is and all that she believes' (DV 8). Tradition is the on-going life of the community. It is the communal wisdom and experience of the whole Church. The function of the magisterium is to interpret authoritatively what is in the content of revelation.

We are in line with true living tradition when we re-interpret the articles of faith. The gospel figure of Jesus was a first interpretation by the infant Church of the Jesus who had been seen and experienced in history. In the fifth century Chalcedon re-thought and re-expressed the Church's faith in the same Jesus and safeguarded the scriptural data concerning him. In the thirteenth century St Thomas undertook to re-think the faith in terms of his day, and his views prevailed for centuries. In the sixteenth century the Council of Trent safeguarded the faith at the time of the Reformation. The Council fathers translated the past dogmatic statements into the categories of thought of their day.

We are called upon to take our place in a long line of witnesses to the faith. In the past dogmas arose because Christians in real historical situations re-acted to the culture of their day. They found themselves in a position where they had to preserve the gospel message from attack or from falling into superstition. They met the needs of their day with the methods of their day. If we want to be responsible men of our time we cannot evade the task of re-thinking and re-formulating our dogmas. We are compelled to this for various reasons. Christians today are constantly being faced with doubts and disputes, and the Church must express its beliefs more precisely and authoritatively in order to exclude some particular error. Besides this, the Church as a whole can grow in understanding of the truths of faith as a result of wider knowledge and deeper experience, and it will be led to give testimony to this new understanding by means of a re-formulation of its doctrine. For example, the central fact of the life, death and resurrection of Jesus is unchanging, but our view of the significance of that central fact can change and deepen. Thus in the last few decades the biblical sciences have given us a fuller knowledge of Jesus' teaching whilst the social and behavioural sciences have given a fuller understanding of what it means to be human, and consequently we may be expected to express differently our understanding of Jesus, the God-man. Instead of repeating traditional statements we have to re-think them taking into account the very different way of looking at the world that has developed as a result of the greater knowledge we have acquired thanks to the physical and human sciences. For example, the theologians at the moment are re-thinking the doctrine of original sin and trying to keep what is essential in the formulation of the Council of Trent.

In our effort to preserve and hand on what we have received, the past definitions retain a normative role. What our forefathers said in the creeds and dogmatic formulations expressed certain truths which must be preserved. We cannot break with tradition either for the sake of being modern or for the sake of going right back to the New Testament as if all the intervening development could be left out. The creeds and the beliefs of the early councils cannot be set aside without destroying the continuing identity of the Christian community. The authentic truths which our forefathers expressed are unchanging, but if we are to grasp those ancient truths we have to re-think them. We have to ask ourselves: if the Church expressed this dogma in this way in the cultural, conceptual framework of that age, how do we express the same reality in our contemporary situation? Thus we recognize the control that must be exercised over our attempts at doctrinal formulations. Those past definitions contain statements of essential aspects of the gospel which we do not want to distort or dilute. They have a normative role, but they have to be reinterpreted if the tradition is to be carried on responsibly as a living tradition.

It is recognized by pastoral-minded teachers that unless such updating of dogmas takes place many Christians, especially the young, will give up professing the faith. Our students today, with their scientific mentality, have a very different way of looking at the world. They tend to accept only what they can test and verify by scientific methods. They are suspicious — and rightly so — of two worlds, the world of faith and the world around us. Much of the old teaching has given the impression of some separate sacred world in which we come in contact with God. With the excessive distinction between sacred and secular, it suggests an unreal world alongside this material one in which we live.

Moreover, Catholics in general are much more critically-minded than they used to be, and they find it difficult to fall in with some of the demands of traditional Catholicism. Traditional Catholicism demands that we should be passively submissive to authority, that we should find the fullness of saving truth in a limited number of sacred sources (Church and Bible), and that we should adhere to a deposit of faith completed centuries ago. But our generation has been brought up to think critically rather than blindly accept a body of truths authoritatively imposed on them; they take it for granted that we should be ready to change and correct our ideas by dialogue with people who do not think like ourselves, and that we make ourselves receptive to the contributions of every group of men, including atheists and agnostics.

If the Church continues to resist the valid standard of modern critical thought Catholicism will dwindle to a small band of reactionaries plus those who like to be told what to believe without having to think for themselves. But fortunately, the Vatican Council has shown that the Church does not want to resist the movement towards change yet at the same time it will not yield to *all* the demands of modernity. We are not to drop or adulterate one fragment of the gospel. Nevertheless, as modern men we can and must disengage the gospel from every antiquated world-view and culturally conditioned ideology. The contemporary Christian need not look upon the world with the eyes of a first century Jew or a mediaeval churchman. If he is a man of strong faith he will be humble enough to criticize the presuppositions of his beliefs and to learn from the sciences of the present day. By continually improving upon previous formulations, he may gain deeper insights into the mystery of Christ.

F. SOMERVILLE

Freedom of faith and R.E.

Freedom is one of those things which are at one and at the same time most attacked in the contemporary world and most highly valued. There is a strange paradox here. On the one hand you have the psychologist, particularly the behaviourist psychologist and the neurologist, examining the ways in which man's behaviour is controlled by external pressure to such an extent that to some of these men the very title 'freedom of faith' would have no meaning at all. On the other hand, you have a tremendous sensitivity in the modern world to freedom of expression, freedom of the press, freedom to meet, freedom to be oneself. A writer like Carl Rogers can say: 'Evidence from therapy, from subjective living and from objective research shows that personal freedom and responsibility have a crucial significance, that one cannot live a complete life without such personal freedom and responsibility, and that self-understanding and personal choice make a sharp and measurable difference to the behaviour of the individual.' So, as I say, we have the strange paradox that the world on the one hand seems almost to deny the very possibility of freedom, and on the other hand cherishes it most highly. Perhaps one could say that one key to the paradox is to remind ourselves that freedom is in essence not freedom from external pressures, but essentially an inner thing. Victor Frankl, writing of his experiences in a concentration camp, speaks of the way in which in the circumstances of a concentration camp, all those things that normally constitute the dignity of a man are taken from him; he no longer has a name; he is called by a number; all his personal possessions are taken from him. He has no status. And yet there is something which no one can touch: the essential freedom which is his inner freedom. He says that the last human freedom is to choose one's attitude in any given set of circumstances, the freedom to choose one's way. All of us have at some time or other experienced in our lives the situation of being caught as it were in a context of circumstances over which we have no control. They are there as factors in a situation; and yet we exercise our freedom in making our own personal decision in the context of all those circumstances. We cannot free ourselves from them because they are there; but we determine ourselves within them. A Dutch magazine some years back told the story of an airman who was shot down during the war; he came down in home territory, but he was very badly damaged in the process, and he had to have both legs amputated. The surgeon was very anxious that when he regained sufficient consciousness to become aware of what had happened to him, this news should be broken to him by someone who could do it gently and with great understanding, because the man was only twenty one. It was an Anglican chaplain who performed this task, and he wrote afterwards of his own trepidation as he drove to the hospital wondering how on earth he was going to break this news to the young man. They talked a little while — the boy obviously did not know what had happened to him — and finally he brought the conversation round to the subject of the injuries he had suffered and the chaplain said, putting it very simply and very briefly: 'You know I have to tell you that they have taken your legs'. And the boy answered: 'They have not taken my legs. I have given them'. And that is the difference between compulsion and freedom. It reminds us perhaps of the words of the gospel: 'No man takes my life from me; I lay it down of myself'. This helps us to understand something of the essential nature of freedom. Again, Carl Rogers, who writes of this very sensitively: 'It is the quality of courage which enables a person to step into the uncertainty of the unknown as he chooses himself. It is the discovery of meaning from within oneself, meaning which comes from listening sensitively and openly to the complexities of what one is experiencing. It is the burden of being responsible for the self one chooses to be. It is the recognition of a person that he is an emerging process, not a static product. The individual who is thus deeply and courageously thinking his own thoughts, becoming his own uniqueness, responsibly choosing himself, may be fortunate in having hundreds of objective outer alternatives from which to choose or he may be unfortunate in having none, but his freedom exists regardless'.

Freedom then is not an absence of external pressures. It is an inner liberty by which a man determines himself.

We have tended to think as follows. Johnny comes into the

school system at the age of five. He has faith because he has been baptized. The criterion almost of our religious education is that he should keep the faith. But scripture does not talk either about keeping or losing faith, but does talk a great deal about growing in faith. It is a static concept of faith that considers it as something put into us at baptism, which we can lose as we can lose a railway ticket; and above all as something we must cling to and keep. This kind of thinking has entered into the way we assess religious education; for instance the criterion for a successful course in religious education would be that Johnny keeps the faith. And if he lacks it or loses it, we come to one of three conclusions: either he has lost it through his own fault because he is lazy or obstinate or something like that; or he has lost it because he has been subject to strong influences from his peer group or his parents; or we have failed in our task as religious educators. We would come to one of these three conclusions. But if we take the freedom of faith seriously, if we see faith not as a static thing but something that grows dynamically with the reaction between the call of God and the answer of man constantly throughout life, if we see it that way and think seriously of the freedom of faith, we shall realize that Johnny at the age of five is not sufficiently free to make an act of faith. I am not saying that he has not received already from the community a disposition to faith. But in terms of an act of faith, a boy of five is not sufficiently free to make an act of faith. We are not born free. It is a fallacy to say we are. We are born with a right to freedom. It belongs to our human nature. But we are not in fact born free. A tiny baby is very unfree, the slave of its instincts; it has to be. If it were not, it would not suck and it would die. It just has to be the slave of its instincts so that it can survive. We freely become free. It is a long job; and it is not finished for any of us yet.

To realize that faith must be a free action implies an effort in education to increase a person's area of freedom. And once you have said that, you have to stop and say: honestly, has that been the objective of our religious education? We shall never have absolute freedom. We cannot. But to the degree to which we are free, so we become more and more capable of a true act of faith.

Now in terms of education, this, I think, confronts us with a kind of dilemma. The same dilemma occurs in relation to

moral education. Quite apart from religious education and faith,
a similar dilemma occurs once you start to consider the nature
of a moral act and the necessity of freedom for morality. John
Wilson in his *Introduction to Moral Education* speaks of this
dilemma in moral education. He calls it the dilemma which has
troubled both practical and theoretical educationists. This
dilemma arises from a feeling of tension between two desires,
on the one hand the desire to ensure that our children have a
solid framework within which to live, perhaps a faith to live by,
and that we do not let them run wild, thereby losing the advantages of a process of socialization which has been built up over
many generations, and, on the other hand, a desire not to
indoctrinate or condition, sometimes expressed as an unwilling-
ness to interfere with their natural development. So we are
caught: on the one hand we realize there is something in the
inheritance which is theirs, the whole structure of society
and the protection of law and obedience and discipline which
protects a child before he is able to exercise mature and complete freedom, and we must not rob him of that degree of
support which is what helps him towards greater freedom. On
the other hand we are afraid of indoctrination, of conditioning,
of preventing true growth to freedom. And the same sort of
dilemma comes into religious education. It works itself out in
two extremes we can fall into. In our system of education in the
past we have tended to fall into the first extreme: to concentrate
on the inculcating of religious practices and dogmas, to discourage questioning and enquiry. Heresy-hunting and what I
call a spiritual excommunication belong to this mentality; and
its aim was protective, given the kind of understanding of
freedom that we had and the way in which we judged the success
of true faith or true religion by conformity rather than by
sincerity. That is the one extreme. And the other extreme is that
of *laissez-faire*, an abdication of responsibility for the learning
situation and an abdication of the Christian witness. We say that
the children have got to be free, they have to find their own
way, and so we let them do it. We leave them to it. That is the
other extreme. And neither of these extremes is true to what we
understand by faith, the growth of faith and the freedom of
faith.

The degree of freedom which we possess as human beings

comes slowly to us; it comes with the process of maturation. A child is introduced at birth into a group, and this group must be a sustaining community for that child. Certain values are communicated early to the child by the attitudes, dispositions and practices of the group. This is right and proper. You just could not eliminate all these influences upon him. It is false to think that anyone must not be influenced. You and I have been influenced over and over again in the course of our lives. This does not diminish our freedom. In fact we grow in reaction to and in response to the many influences that come to bear upon us. No man can exist free from influences. Life is constantly receiving from others, and this does not destroy freedom. So we must not go to the extreme of thinking that in order for a person to be free he must have no mention of religion made to him until he is able to choose his own faith. This is inhuman. It is not true to the way we are.

Another way in which this extreme is expressed is that a number of people, particularly Catholics who are waking up to the seriousness of faith, are so convinced of it now that they begin to be afraid of making any statement to a child of their own faith. I will come back to this in a moment.

What is it that makes an act of faith free? It is the freedom of the person. My act of faith will be free in proportion to the degree that I am free. So we want in our educational system to help children and young people to become more and more free. What are the things from which we can help them to become free? I will enumerate only some of the factors from which we want to help them to be liberated. One freedom we want for them is freedom from ignorance, which is a limit to man's freedom. This does not mean that knowledge alone liberates. Nevertheless freedom from ignorance is important and we ought not to be afraid of the truth. I sometimes think we are. Surely the truth need never be feared. If the truth seems to question something that we hold very dear, we should have enough faith in truth to go forward and look at this truth and not put it under the carpet. We must not think that man is a purely rational creature. The longer I live the less I think man is a rational creature. We are not moved to action by reason. Without, therefore, the exaggeration of a purely intellectual approach to religious education, we do know the importance of freedom from ignorance.

We must free from fear and guilt. This is where we do need
to examine our consciences because a certain amount of
education has been an attempt to control behaviour by fear. The
danger today is more that we should control behaviour by
psychological expertise. Unfortunately, we have used fear and
guilt to control behaviour. In its simplest form this sort of
control is exerted by the mother who says to her child: 'You're
a naughty boy. Will you behave yourself? God will not love
you if you behave like that'. That, objectively speaking, is
blasphemy; and it is a terrible thing to say to a child.
But we have used guilt feelings and fear to control
behaviour. This is not religion and not freedom of faith. On the
other hand, freedom from fear and guilt is not the same as
irresponsibility. A man is not truly free if he is irresponsible;
for this means ignoring the realities of life and the consequences
of one's action, whereas a free decision is taken in full knowledge
of these consequences. For example, in a counselling situation it
is not diminishing a person's freedom to help him to know the
consequences of any decision he will make. It increases his area
of freedom to do this. So freedom from fear and guilt is not
irresponsibility.

We want to free from the tyranny of law. Again within the
whole history of religion you will find the struggle against the
tendency to idolize law in a sense, to set up the law as an
absolute. But the law is never an absolute. The whole of the
gospel and much of St Paul have much to say about the Spirit of
Christ freeing us from the dominion of the law. At the same
time freedom from law does not mean anarchy. Anarchy is not
a help to freedom. A human being in a situation of anarchy is
not free, because he is then the victim of power. Sometimes
young teachers and students in colleges of education who are
responsive to the notion of freedom and keen to use discussion
methods in the classroom, begin to think that all they have to do
is to sit back in the classroom and let the pupils discuss. They
forget that if you are showing a film to children in order to
stimulate discussion they will not get very far if they spend the
half hour throwing books at one another. In order that there be
free discussion there must be order, not anarchy. The leader in
this situation is the custodian of this degree of order; the task
of the teacher is to ensure and maintain a learning situation. So

once again we have to avoid the two extremes: one extreme being to govern by law and the other being to abandon one's responsibility if one happens to be in authority. The maintenance of a learning situation is in order that each member of the group shall be free really to express himself and to be heard.

The last freedom of the four I want to mention is freedom from compulsion, from pressure, from power structures, from authority in the sense of authoritativeness. But this does not mean an absence of support. It does not mean a failure to communicate concern. It does not mean a fear to witness. To testify to my own faith is not a threat to the freedom of another if I fully respect the other. If you have a relationship with adolescents which is such that they know you respect them and their opinions, they will want to know what your opinions are. If you think they have no right to any opinion other than yours, you have lost them. But I have yet to meet a group of adolescents who have not listened with deep respect to a convinced person who has respect for their convictions. This helps us in the present transformation of the approach to religious education. If we encourage free discussion in a classroom or a group of adolescents and if we maintain a position of neutrality during a discussion, and if our total concern seems to be to maintain a learning situation, then outside this particular exercise we ourselves remain absolutely free to express our own convictions when the group so desires it, without any fear of limiting the freedom of that group. I would go further and say that in the situation of religious education in which we are engaged we betray the group if we do not do that. If we are afraid because we have some strange fear of limiting their freedom in this rather mistaken way, if we are afraid to say what it is we believe in, then we are betraying these youngsters who want to know. This is the kind of balance we have to work for, which makes it possible to bear testimony to our own faith without in any way hindering the growth of another; the condition seems to me to be to respect the dignity of every human being with whom we are in dialogue, and to hold fast to the conviction, which will come ultimately from our own experience of growth, of the nature of faith and its essential freedom.

SISTER RUTH DUCKWORTH

An anthropological approach in catechetics

Some disquiet is being felt among a number of parents and teachers about the content and method of religious teaching in our schools. They fear that the great doctrines of God, Christ and the Church such as are summarized in the 'penny' catechism are not being taught as fully or as explicitly as they should be. They complain that the children spend too much time in the religion class upon activities which seem to have no connection with religion; teaching methods seem to have become secularized. Here it is intended to consider only one aspect of the anxiety which some people have expressed, the place of the study of man in religious education. Some older people, who cherish the instruction they received at school, make the charge that the renewalists in catechetics seem to be moving away from the study of God to the study of man, and are in effect promoting an anaemic form of humanism with faint Christian overtones.

Anthropology

Anthropology is a fashionable word at the moment. It means the study of man as an animal and as a member of society. Traditionally this science had primitive peoples as its principal subject matter. Since the nineteenth century, however, it has extended its scope to cover man in literate and industrial societies; and the distinction between this science and sociology is becoming less clearly defined. Much attention has been paid to the study of man, especially by atheists and humanists who have no use for the study of God, and who have undoubtedly added greatly to our knowledge of man. Their prestige stands high. Consequently, one hears it said that Catholic theologians and teachers are so desirous to be 'with it' that they are trying to meet these men on their own ground to the neglect of certain traditional religious truths.

There is perhaps a grain of truth that Catholic theologians have been influenced by the social scientists. The task of theology is to reflect upon faith and try to express it in clear coherent language. In order to do this properly it must take into account the findings of anthropology, psychology and sociology. Most probably the work of the experts in these various sciences has made theologians realize how they had neglected man and they now seek to make up for the deficiency.

Theological reasons

Whatever may have been the *occasion* of their recent concentration on the study of man, theologians have discovered that they must make this study much more fully than in the past for the sake of sound theology. Various reasons impel them to this pursuit.

First we have come to a better understanding of what revelation is. It is not, as we once taught, so much a set of truths communicated by God and passed on from generation to generation, as rather an on-going process initiated by God who enters into communication with men whom he treats as friends. God 'speaks' to men in history, and just as our speaking does not reveal us unless someone listens and reacts in some way, so God's self-revelation is not revelation unless man receives it and responds in some way. Man's acceptance (or repudiation) is part of the revelation. Revelation is an I-Thou relationship, God speaking and man responding. Consequently, it is supremely important that we also study man, the other term of the revelation relationship. Man listens to other people, and through these others he is able to listen to the world, to history and to God. In religious education then, 'we should at least spend as much time thinking about the receivers of God's word as we do about the doctrine itself' (A conclusion of the Manila Catechetical Study Week).

If God speaks, as we believe, in the events, needs and aspirations of men today, then the religious educator along with

E

his students must become acquainted with those contemporary events, needs and desires. He must look and listen to the world of today and read the signs of the times in the light of Jesus Christ, God's first and last word.

We now realize that theology in the past has studied chiefly the mystery of God in himself without sufficient attention to the consequences for man. For example, when theologians discussed the Blessed Trinity they treated it as a matter of relations between the divine persons. But the mystery was surely revealed for our information and living; so it must have something to throw light on man himself. Another example is the distinction that has been made, practically to the point of separation, between nature and supernature, which in turn has led to a divorce between nature and grace, between the world of man and the world of grace. But, in fact, grace permeates all aspects of daily existence.

The old style theology has been reflected in Christian spirituality. Spiritual writers have tended to depreciate earthly values, to advocate aloofness from the world, to think that holiness came from praying but not from playing, to exalt the greatness of God at the expense of stressing the insignificance of man. The reaction against such theology and spirituality was endorsed by the Second Vatican Council, especially in *The Church in the Modern World*, which discerned the positive values in what may appear superficially as secular trends among men, and the same reaction is expressed in the present theological concern for the joys and hopes, griefs and anxieties of men today.

Finally, though one could add further reasons for the study of man in theology and religious education, the scriptures provide a theological anthropology. A work like A. Gelin's *The Concept of Man in the Bible* shows how the Old Testament sees man as a living personal individual unity (not body plus soul), a member of a community, a creature of God, responsible for his acts, conscious of himself as sinful yet hopeful of salvation. In the New Testament Jesus Christ is the new man of the Old Testament promises. Jesus himself in his teaching does not portray the ideal man. Rather he takes man in the concrete circumstances of every day life. He preaches that men must love their neighbour, and therein find salvation. St Paul looks at man in the light of Christ's death-resurrection. He contrasts man before the coming of Christ (unredeemed) and as he is in Christ (redeemed), man as he was under the law and now in faith, man as he was under the dominion of sin and now as a child of God. We have, therefore, in sacred scripture, the highest precedent for a theological and catechetical study of man.

A theology of man

The physicists study man as a part of the matter-energy system; the biologists study him as an organism assimilating vegetation and reproducing his kind; psychologists as an organism subject to basic needs and drives; sociologists as a leader or follower within the structure of social organization; economists as a producer and consumer of goods and services; philosophers as a rational animal. Their various contributions have given us a quite considerable knowledge of man or growth in self-understanding. But more important than all these is the work of the theologian who studies man in terms of his relationship with God and incorporates within a theological perspective the findings of the other specialists. Unfortunately, we do not yet possess a theology of man, an intelligible coherent understanding of man in responsible relation to God. We have hundreds of notions from which we form our own concept of man, a concept which upon analysis would be found to be full of unverifiable assumptions. For example, we ourselves may be among those who take a pessimistic view of man, convinced that he is radically sinful, selfish and weak, a creature to whom the grace of God comes as a saving balm. Or we may be among those who take an optimistic view: God's creation is good despite the 'fall', and man tends by nature towards goodness, fulfilment and self-transcendence. Or perhaps we take up a middle position saying that there is an ambiguity inherent in human nature: man endures contradictory experiences, and in consequence exists in a state of tension between flesh and spirit. All three concepts will be found underlying catechetical themes treated by authors and some of them lead to unwarrantable assertions about

human nature. We stand in need of a sound Christian theology
of man.

From man to faith

A person may agree that it is desirable to have a fuller
treatment of man than the one we used to receive apropos
of the creation of Adam. But he may question whether,
as a matter of method in theology and catechetics, it is legitimate
to start from man to rise to the mystery of faith. We think that
it is, for three reasons. First, on the ground that supernature
presupposes nature the religious educator must know the
individual to whom he is talking. He knows what religious truth
he wants to teach, but he must give thought to the concrete
situation in which the student lives: his relation to others, his
belonging to a community, his relation to nature. The educator
must also know himself, since we all have our prejudices and
shortcomings, and he can unwittingly falsify religious truth.
Secondly, the revealed Christian message, known by faith, must
be seen to be credible if it is to be accepted. Now a thing is
credible to a person if it responds to some interest or need he
feels or if it satisfies his reason. The religious educator appeals
to the desire for happiness that dwells in every man and shows
him how the Christian message, good news, gives deep significance to that desire and throws light on it. Thirdly, the
Christian message is also a call to conversion, a summons to
leave behind a former mentality and way of life in order to enter
on a new way. This does not mean you leave your physical
environment, but you stay where you are and live differently.
Consequently, one must know, as was said above, the concrete
situations in which men are in order to learn from what condition
they are to turn away.

Finally in order to know God we must know man. The
human is the medium and the only medium of the divine. God
does not reveal himself directly since he is spirit and invisible
and we are bound by the senses. He communicates with us
through intermediaries: the events of human history, our human
relationships, and above all the human nature of Jesus Christ.
God is in Jesus Christ. This is why the manhood of Jesus is so
necessary and important for us; it is the only place for us where

God is to be found. And we know about Christ's manhood not only from the fragmentary gospel narratives, but still more from the study of what being human means in ourselves. The starting point in all religious teaching will have to be some understanding of ourselves from which we move to an understanding of Jesus Christ, the one mediator, who leads us to the God in whom we live and move and have our being.

F. SOMERVILLE

As man is

In a fairly recent lecture I caused quite a jolt when I said that profession of vows or ordination to the priesthood is not intended to make people more religious but to make them more human. Yet the same can be said of the whole Christian endeavour, of all our teaching and of all our catechizing; for to be human is to measure up to the full stature of the humanity of Christ. Here at once is God's basic invitation to man and man's life-long challenge and responsibility. Man is alone the creature created and called by God to assume full responsibility for himself and fashion his own destiny. Whenever he relinquishes this unique privilege of his he ceases to be man. Kierkegaard recognized this and declared that the only real sin is 'the despairing refusal to be oneself'. It is, in a word, the refusal to love and this, in fact, according to the Bible, is what sin is all about.

It is a pity that for so long concentration on the account of Adam's fall as the beginning of all sin has succeeded in blinding people to the intention and importance of the whole first section of Genesis. The stories of Cain and Abel, of Noah and the Ark, and of the Tower of Babel are just as forceful as the Garden of Eden story in symbolising the character of man's sin. All these stories illustrate after their own manner the devious ways in which man abdicates his assignment to live up to his essential humanity, that is, to live in love and in the spirit of brotherhood.

But our main concern here is not so much man's response or his failure to respond. We are concerned rather with man himself: what kind of being he is to whom the divine invitation has been issued and what are the main factors influencing him as a person and therefore determining to some extent at least his response; what is it that helps or hinders him in the unending process of his own self-creation?

A body-spirit unity

Man, first of all, is a *psychosomatic* being — an embodied spirit if you like, a creature composed of body and spirit, intrinsically one and entirely unique.

This body-spirit composition is of first importance in any consideration of man, because it immediately puts him on a plane apart from all the rest of creation. It points to a very special type of being who alone is capable of full human response to stimuli affecting him from within and from without. Man must not be looked upon as a spirit imprisoned in a material body which accompanies him through life as a necessary evil, always impeding to some extent his highest spiritual aspirations. Nor are soul and body to be identified. The point is though, there is continuous interpretation and interaction between the two; their distinct activities are mutually related and so can never really be dissociated.

It is, as we have just inferred, because man is an embodied spirit that he is unique amongst all God's creatures. Being made in the image and likeness of God who is *Love,* man's fundamental power is his indefinable power to love. It is this that constitutes him a person. His capacity to love derives from his nature as a free being who can choose to love or not to love, to give himself in love to another, or to withhold, withdraw, isolate himself and, therefore, destroy the gift that he is.

We know from experience that man is endowed with what is usually called free will — the liberty, in other words, by which he can to a certain degree order and plan his own life. For example, he chooses to get up in the morning rather than to stay in bed; to eat, to study, to go about his daily work; or, he can obstinately refuse to do these and countless other things. This, after all, is one of the big difficulties with man, that from the time of his creation right down through the centuries of history, he has done many things that he ought not to have done but, much more significantly, he has left undone those things that he ought to have done. He has refused to live up to the dignity of his manhood.

This possibility of choice is clearly perceptible even in the child we teach — before ever, in fact, he reaches school-going age at all. But the child is still very immature and, therefore, incapable of exercising true liberty. In this sense some people remain 'children' all their lives. Well, then, we might ask, how is true liberty achieved? How does one attain to that maturity which is apparently necessary for the exercise of freedom?

In order to be truly human, personal liberty must be directed by something deeper, more stable and more complete. It must be sustained and oriented by a profound and total commitment — a response of the whole person in love, what is called today a *fundamental option* in which the person expresses himself fully with all that he wills to be in this life in relation to the world, to people, to God. But this type of fundamental option becomes possible only as the result of a long, slow process of maturation in time. It is expressed only in time. Maturity and, therefore, true freedom, are not something which we acquire once and for all — say at a certain age — but something which we go on acquiring throughout the course of our whole life.

An historical being

This opens up to us a further consideration of man which, in the school-room or outside of it, we can never afford to forget. It is this, that man is an *historical being*. He is never what he is at any given moment of his earthly existence. His past and future are of vital importance in any assessment of the human being as well as of human action. There is a sense, for example, as we have just implied, in which man is not free but freely becomes free. Again, we never arrive. We are forever arriving, because the human condition is situated in time and is inevitably borne along by the flux of history. God's invitation continually takes account of the particular state of a person's development at a given time or in a given situation. We, as teachers, are much less willing than God is to make allowance for the slowness of psychological and historical maturation, forgetting that we ourselves are part of the self-same process; that tomorrow, for example, we shall be different from what we are today and, hopefully, that we shall also be better persons.

Man can respond only gradually to God's invitation. He may be totally blind to what is demanded of him, or, he may be misunderstanding or even rejecting the divine invitation, and so he must now be brought forward step by step. This applies to adults as well as to children, to whole communities as well as to particular persons. Child and adult, person and community, are all subjects of historical development and can suffer from retardation which to a greater or lesser degree curtails knowledge, inhibits personal responsibility, impedes human action and conditions human response.

Every activity of ours on the contrary that fully responds to the truth or the reality of what we are, opens up to us new horizons — new powers of freedom — by which we become what we are, persons. And this is our basic vocation, the work of a life-time.

But how are teachers to get this across to their students? To talk to a young person about being himself, or about becoming what he is, could be very misleading especially if the educator — teacher or parent — is not clear in his own mind about what exactly this means or involves.

Each of us is the product of our past experiences, our physical and mental limitations, and above all of our past decisions. But we are as yet an unfinished product. At every moment I am creating the person that I choose to be. Whatever my limitations, whatever my past, I hold myself in my own hands at every moment to mould and fashion as I decide. To become what I am, then, does not amount to uncovering the sort of self that I was born or fated to be. It means *discovering my own true freedom* to fashion myself as I can and as I will. This consideration is in itself an eye-opener to the responsibility resting with each person in regard to himself, but also to the responsibility which as educators we have in regard to our young people.

It is surely the task of education, and especially of religious education, to point to Christian values as worthy of attainment, values by which a person's whole future can be governed to the extent that he really grasps and personalizes them. The emphasis here is on training in personal responsibility — for one's own life first of all and, in addition as we shall see presently, for the lives of others. Our pupils must be trained to see that their destiny consists precisely in the formation of that self which they themselves create with every new decision deriving from personal freedom. It is I who at every moment decide what sort of person I shall be, and this is my human dignity. To be myself is to be free.

Equally important and inescapable is the other side of the coin which tells the truth that man can distort his own growth process. He can interrupt and impede it, turn it away from its true end and empty it of meaning by a kind of spiritual atrophy which he freely accepts under the pressures and disillusions of life. In other words, the fundamental option which we have been stressing here is psychologically conditioned by the influence of others.

A community being

And now we come to the third and last point — *man's community dimension*. The emphasis on person and community in recent years has almost become prosaic. And yet there is still a great deal of confusion in people's minds about these two concepts as if to emphasize the one were automatically to exclude the other. On the contrary, however, person and community are interrelated, correlative realities which cannot be divorced one from the other without damaging and distorting both.

Community is not a collectivity of some sort. If it were, then any amorphous group could be called a community. But this would not satisfy the demands of community at all. Nor is a community a matter of 'togetherness', or even of 'belongingness'. It is essentially a relationship-centred reality. How often in the Church have we not, to our discredit, mistaken physical juxtaposition for real community? It has spared us the trouble of trying to relate to people that we naturally dislike and would prefer to ignore. Practical charity has never been very easy. The old pulpit cliché that 'you must love everybody without necessarily having to LIKE everybody', has come to the rescue and left us with a quiet conscience if not an enlightened one. But the Second Vatican Council has caused us to re-think our position by putting before us a new and challenging ideal of what we are intended to be by reason of the fact itself that we have been made in God's own image and likeness: 'a people made one with the unity of the Father, the Son and the Holy Spirit' (cf. LG n. 4).

This perhaps has been a digression but a necessary one, I think. What has it all got to do with our principal concern here, namely, the kind of being man is who is addressed by God and called to respond to him?

Man is linked to others physically and psychologically by receiving and giving. Both are important. He is born into a community context and immediately becomes part of a whole network of interpersonal relationships where he is subject to influences surrounding him on all sides. His temperament and character, for example, will be conditioned by hereditary factors, by his family and national culture; in a word, by the atmosphere or environment into which he is born and in which he grows up. The breath that he breathes, the body that is his, the name by which he is known, the language that he speaks: all these are given to him by others. Throughout his whole life he stands in constant need of others. 'The deepest need of man', Erich Fromm insists, 'is the need to overcome his separateness, to leave the prison of his aloneness'.

God, in whose image we are made, is love and so love in one way or another is, and must be, the fulfilling of the personality. Life without love is a disunited and impossible kind of existence. That is why fundamentally 'to be' is 'to be with others'. It is, as somebody has said, that 'we' of interpersonal relationships that creates the 'I'. Man is therefore at once independent and interdependent. In isolation he is incomplete. Separation and isolation are the source of all sorts of anxiety and mental disturbances. It is frightening but true that others hold my human maturity in their power — in the sense that alone and unaided I can never become myself. There is no such person as a self-made person who stands outside of community, isolated and insulated.

From the point of view therefore of Christian education, environmental influences are a major consideration. There are powerful forces at work in society moulding and directing the lives and development of our young people and influencing their personal response much more effectively than what we do in school. But our ability to cope with these forces depends to a very large extent on our understanding of the child's home situation, and our perception of the force and value of the more intimate aspects of interpersonal relationships. We can never hope to understand the child in isolation: he must be seen in the context of his home, and of the larger community where his home is situated, if really we are to help him to develop as a person capable of free choice, responsible decision, and loving response within the community of mankind.

The child's community environment, we must remember, is infected to a greater or lesser degree by sin. Christian values have been largely undermined or overthrown. All this is affecting the child and determining his response as a person — not just his present response but his whole future as well. How we are to deflect these influences is the problem and challenge confronting us as educators. As I see it, it involves us in the difficult but essential task of extending Christian education beyond the classroom or school. We must somehow reach out into real life, into the home and family circle.

But this is a sore point and teachers generally can become very self-defensive the moment it is mentioned. A sister, not very long ago, was complaining vehemently to me about the conduct of some of her pupils — all of whom came from more or less the same locality and the same social background. I happened to know the homes of two of those children. I asked the sister if she were aware of the home situation, or if she knew the parents. 'Oh no!' she said, quite indignantly, 'there's no time for that. And anyway, we're an "enclosed" Order. We don't go out.' I could not help replying: 'Forgive my saying so, Sister, but quite obviously then you ought not to be teaching at all.' Of course sisters — in or out of so-called enclosed orders — are not the only delinquents in this respect. It is the problem of time, teachers everywhere will tell you. I think it is much more truly a problem of basic attitudes: how we see our vocation as educators; what understanding we have of the demands of Christian dedication; what value we attach to the human person and the full flowering of personality. We can, alas!, so easily hide behind our profession or specialization for fear of any real involvement. Christianity can make terrible demands upon us. And then it is the old, old story: 'I have married a wife. . . . I've bought a piece of land . . .' or, more tragic still, 'I've become a religious and I have my religious life to live as well'. . . and so on!

But to get back to Christianity: in its deepest sense it does not consist in a creed or code, which is not to deny that these too have their value. In its innermost essence Christianity is commitment to a PERSON — to Christ. It is therefore a way of living — with God, with people, with experience. The religious educator then must see to it that religion is not looked upon as a separate activity, but an activity that runs through the whole of life, and is capable of assimilating every experience and event that come its way. Religious education, if it is to have any meaning or relevance at all, must take place within the relationship of people as persons, because this is what life is all about. Personal existence is by its very nature life with and for others. Religious or Christian education, then, must be capable of gathering into itself the whole of life, of embracing a person's entire future, the future of the world, the future of man.

Conclusion

To sum up, man to whom God's invitation is addressed, is a free, self-conscious, independent and interdependent being, made to the image of God and therefore endowed with a unique human dignity. In issuing his invitation God takes account of man's psychosomatic condition, his historical and community dimensions. Loving interpersonal relationships are an essential part of the response of love to which God calls the human person. In so far as the person responds to this invitation he is radically transformed and raised to an ever closer, more intimate share in the life and love of the tripersonal God — a life of complete and unlimited self-giving.

And so the recognition and fulfilment of the true needs of our students as persons at every stage of their psychological, historical and interpersonal development is the essential task with which all Christian education must grapple. It is an arduous task but one which confronts the genuinely dedicated teacher, not as a difficulty but, as a *challenge*: a challenge which brings the best out of all of us and ends up by so enriching and ennobling us that eventually we ourselves emerge as the first beneficiaries!

SISTER ROSE PATRICIA MCHUGH

Man, the image of God

God created man, says the Bible, in his own image. All men, whether unbelieving, pagan or christian, are made to his image.

No doubt the purpose of this revelation made to the Hebrews and to Christians is to indicate man's special relation to the Creator. If the teacher bears in mind this central truth he can never restrict himself to a merely humanistic study of man. For the doctrine contained here shows that man cannot be understood apart from his special relation to God. Ignorance of it necessarily results in man's misunderstanding of his own nature. The doctrine also shows the uniqueness of man; for however much he may be part of material creation, he is distinguished from the rest as the one whose specific character is to be in the image of God. Again, this doctrine is the real basis for the dignity of each and every individual; whilst remembering the utter distinction between the Creator and creature, we can truly assert in man a real affinity to God.

The scriptural basis

The whole point of Genesis 1 becomes clear in verses 16ff, when we are told the real purpose of God's work: man, embodied spirit, is created in the image of God. The second chapter gives a different order of events; man is created first and all other things are created for man's sake. If man is formed of the 'dust from the ground' (Gen. 2. 7) he is nevertheless animated by the Lord God's breath or spirit which constitutes him 'a living being' and creates a close personal bond with man. Similarly, whilst the rest of the Old Testament has much to say of man's littleness and weakness, it at the same time affirms his unique dignity and pre-eminence.

In the New Testament St Paul develops the idea of image. For him Christ, the new Adam, is *the* image of God (2 Cor. 4. 4; Col. 1. 15) by which is meant that in Christ we see what God is like. God is Christ-like. Through fellowship with Christ the believer is transformed into the same image (Rom. 8. 29; 1 Cor. 15. 49; 2 Cor. 3. 18; Col. 3. 10).

We are in the true tradition of the Church in making much of man created in God's image. It seems to have been the fundamental view of man held by the fathers of the Church. 'This theme, which not only demonstrates the dignity of man, but comprises all his prerogatives, provided the Fathers with a basis for exploring man, analysing his psychology and demonstrating incontrovertibly that man is truly man only when he transcends himself and returns to the God in whose image he is made' (R. Le Trocquer: *What is Man?* p. 10).

'In our image'

How are we to understand this figurative statement of scripture? In the first place we would do well to notice that it denotes not a static characteristic but a dynamic power given to man which he can exercise and become more like God. Man is not constituted the image of God once for all at birth, but grows in likeness to God through a free conscious responding to God's call throughout life. This is how a man becomes the person that God wants. Can we not see the relevance of this dynamic aspect of the image-idea for teaching adolescents who feel themselves incomplete and unstable? Through fellowship with Christ they become their true selves.

That man is God's image means that he is not closed in on himself; his life is outward-looking. The Bible speaks of God in terms of person; he is a personal God. Man is a person, or better, he becomes a human person by going out to others in love. Person means relatedness to others; it is one term of a relationship, an 'I' or a 'you'. Actually, man has relationships to God, to other men and to non-personal beings. The first of these three is the most fundamental. In my relationship with God I am totally a 'receiver person', since everything comes ultimately from God. And my receiver response to him will be a willingness to receive and a going out to him in faith and love.

In the strength of God's own love and self-giving, a man will go out to all God's children. The neighbour will be loved as oneself, that is, as a person, the image of God.

Man, like God, has the capacity to love. We have only to think of the love between parent and children, brothers and sisters, friend and friend. Not one of us has ever met a person who is totally unloving or unloved. We may recall here the profound truth expressed in the beautiful hymn *Ubi caritas et amor,* wherever there is a real love or an act of love there is God. A loving person reflects the love of God for us and indeed reflects God who is love.

Man in his affinity with God has freedom. A person decides for himself and by himself what he shall be, how he shall act, in what direction he shall develop. We do not develop by following one fixed pattern. As we grow numerous alternatives are presented to us through the ever changing circumstances of daily life, and we make a choice of one of them. By these countless free decisions and free actions which nobody can force on us and whose independence God himself respects, we in a certain sense make ourselves.

Man is like God in that we can know the truth. We have already acquired a wealth of knowledge, and we never stop. We want to know more things and we want to know more deeply what we already know. We continue to search, to inquire, to ask questions and seek explanations. We strive naturally and unconsciously for the possession of all truth, in other words, to be more God-like.

Man, made in the image of his Maker, is creative. He is creative when engaged in painting, carving, making music, singing, ballet-dancing, acting on the stage, drawing, sculpturing, writing poetry or a novel, cooking, dress-making. Think of great names in each of these fields. Man the artist uses his imagination to enter into the feelings and moods of other people or reflects on his own, and expresses his experience in many different ways.

He can combine beauty and usefulness in designing cathedrals, churches, houses. . . . He can create order out of chaos when he clears wasteland to build towns and cities.

In the biblical account the affirmation that God created man in his own image is followed by the divine command to 'subdue the earth'. And man is certainly in the process of doing this.

He first built shelters and developed some kinds of architecture to protect himself against the severities of nature. He developed various arts and crafts by which he shows that he transcends nature. Looking around the world today we see the results of a long and glorious conquest of nature by men, so that the earth may become a more human dwelling place. A man simply touches a switch to bring electrical power into his home. Once he could travel only as far as he could walk; he can now fly to the other end of the world in a few hours. He can sit in his arm-chair at home and watch events in far distant lands. Technology shows the marvellous attainments of men in their dominion over things, and opens up the prospect of a still more wonderful future.

The defacement of the image

Man does not, however, have the complete dominion over nature that can belong to him as the image of God. Scripture gives the one and only explanation for the lack: the reign of sin. The image of God in man can be and has been defaced by sin. It has not developed as fully as it could have done because of man's persistent sinfulness. Through sin men have formed a distorted and destructive self-image and exalted themselves into the place of the Creator. Sin has upset the right relationships with God, their neighbours and nature. Where harmony should prevail, imagination, emotions, physical powers and appetites are infected with a drive towards chaos. Sin affects man's history adversely — wars among peoples instead of mutual love and service, resistance from material creation instead of complete subjection. Nevertheless, the fact of sin is only one side of the story. Jesus Christ, the Son of God, has become man to make of us a new creation. He has restored to us that affinity and loving fellowship with God which was weakened by sin. Any one who joins himself to Christ acquires a sonship like that of the Son, the unique image of the Father. Such a person's mind and will are drawn into the movement of the love that is in God. In Christ man recovers his former place in the midst of creation and is able to rule over it and bring it to a manifestation of the human spirit.

F

Catechetical notes

We need to make much of this fundamental view of man and stress the image-idea as a potentiality rather than a static endowment. By reason of the affinity with God, we can enter into friendship with him. Indeed, we are called to perfecting the friendship, which is the perfection of love, and which we call heaven.

Stress that we reflect our friendship with God by our love and service of our fellowmen in community.

We are also called to be like Jesus Christ, the perfect 'image of the invisible God' (Col. 1. 15). We are to look upon and react to persons and things as Christ does. We are to have 'the mind of Christ' when dealing with others and in coming to grips with the human situations in our own life.

Recall that as the image of God we are to open ourselves to the Spirit of God to perceive and accept truth and goodness and thus grow in the likeness of God in our living and loving.

We should teach that despite sin many signs of the divine image in man remain: personality, power to love, freedom, reason, creativeness, dominion over nature, and above all capacity for fellowship with God.

T. CHAPMAN

The new man

The dream of a golden age seems to have always haunted the minds of men. It is found embodied in many ancient religious myths. The same hope and longing inspires men today in a more realistic way as they continue to strive through scientific and technological progress to build a new world in which all needs and wants will be satisfied. They have already achieved some spectacular conquests and cling to their expectations of still greater advances.

Christians share with their fellowmen these hopes for a new world, and all should work together to promote human progress that will make life more liveable and enjoyable through material prosperity, justice, peace and brotherhood. Whilst they have much in common with others, Christians are inspired by a distinctive world-view and their own idea of the shape of things to come.

Working for a new age

They join in the common effort to build a better world. But they see this as a task entrusted to them by God. They look upon modern development as part of the unfolding of God's creation. God has not made a finished world; he has created the world-process and he has created man in his own image, that is, endowed with creativeness. Men have to take part in the process of continued creation by using their knowledge and skill and thus help bring the universe to completion.

Christians seek human progress; but unlike the materialists they do not subscribe to the illusion of inevitable progress to ever more perfect conditions. They do not hail everything modern as true progress, and, what is more important, they recognize that every phase of progress remains within the limits of the finite and hence will keep us waiting for still further progress without ever reaching the absolute. The final development of this world does not lie in future time, but beyond

time. It will be the new world which in biblical language is
called 'heaven' and 'eternal life'. And this new world comes
not as a human achievement, but as essentially a gift from God.

Moreover, when Christians think of the goal of the new age,
they do not think so much of the physical world, the exterior
conditions of man, although these are not excluded, but primarily of man's own fulfilment. The new man is more important
than the new world. The eternal life just mentioned is
defined by Jesus Christ as 'knowing thee the only true God, and
Jesus Christ whom thou hast sent' (Jn 17. 3), where 'knowing'
is understood in the biblical sense of close acquaintance through
love, such as spouses have of each other. Man is indeed
perfectible, but he will never develop fully all his potentialities
in the present world. His fulfilment will come from God and
shine forth in all its splendour at the end of time.

However, the goal of human hopes and longings is not
entirely in the future. The new life is present even now. The
new man has already come into existence. Jesus Christ has made
all men, however different they are, in himself 'one new man'
(Eph. 2. 15). Those who receive a 'new birth' in the Holy
Spirit (Jn 3. 5-8) are to serve God in a 'new spiritual way'
(Rom 7 6) and walk in 'a newness of life'. They are a 'new
creature' (Gal. 6. 15), living under a 'new commandment'
(Jn 13. 34), and at the end of time there will be for them a 'new
heaven and a new earth' (Apoc. 21. 1). Since this doctrine
accounts for the Christian being at heart an optimist, we had
better examine the sound basis on which it rests.

Christ, the new Adam

Jesus Christ, by his saving work, has renewed mankind with
a new heart and a new spirit as had been announced by the Old
Testament prophets (Jeremiah and Ezekiel). St Paul presents
Christ as the new Adam, the first of a new line of men. In 1 Cor.
15. 21-22, 45-49 the apostle, dealing with a controversy among
the Corinthians, draws an antithesis between the first Adam, a
living being, and Christ, a life-giving spirit. Christ renews everything; he gives new life to all. He is the great turning-point of all
history, since he has turned mankind in the direction of its true

destiny. His destiny is the example and source of ours; Christians share in it. He conquered death by resurrection, and so shall we.

In Rom. 5. 12-21 Paul again makes an analogy and contrast between Adam and Christ. The passage is rich in doctrine, but for our purpose here it is sufficient to note how he shows that sin and death for all men followed upon the first Adam's disobedience whereas acquittal and life followed upon Christ's perfect obedience. Christ is the new Adam, head of the human race now recreated by God.

By the Incarnation the Word became flesh. Jesus Christ is one of us, sharing in every respect our human conditions with the one exception of never having sinned. He lives this life of ours in a new way as he keeps the right relationship with God and his fellowmen. In doing so he begins to turn our human life towards its true destiny. Christ is not only man, he is the new man in whom all the newness of our race is rooted.

The Christian, a new man

The scriptural teaching of Christ as the new Adam is a concrete way of referring to us who are renewed through the influence of the risen life-giving Christ. He is the head of a new race to which he gives life. In him we have new life: 'If any one is in Christ, he is a new creation; the old has passed away and the new has come' (2 Cor. 5. 17).

The transformation into new men is accomplished through faith and baptism. Faith is necessary because man is spirit and the transformation is primarily in the order of spirit: a passing from alienation to friendship with God. Faith is man's response to God's call made through the preaching of the apostles. In the death and resurrection of Jesus God has made known his loving design for all men who are under the power of sin. In the risen Christ the wisdom of God has been made manifest, and the apostles, who let themselves be transformed by the power of the Spirit radiating from the risen Christ, have received the mission to preach this mystery of new life and call men to share in it. And men are to respond by the surrender of faith, a commitment and acceptance of the whole person.

Besides faith, baptism is an element in the transformation of man. In this sacred rite the believer is joined to Christ in his

passing from a sinful condition to new life and shares with him
its consequences. 'If we have been united with him in a death
like his, we shall certainly be united with him in a resurrection
like his' (Rom. 6. 5). When we are baptized we share in his
death and in the newness of life which his resurrection has made
possible for us. The death is a death to sin and the new life is
life to God. Baptized into Christ, Christians 'have put on
Christ' (Gal. 3. 20), they have taken upon themselves the
qualities of Christ, and become the friends of God with all
their sins forgiven (Col. 2. 13). But baptism does not effect only
reconciliation with God, it unites men together in love and does
away with old divisions: 'There is neither Jew nor Greek,
neither slave nor free, neither male nor female; for you are all
one in Christ Jesus' (Gal. 3. 28). In other words, we cannot
talk about one another as being white or coloured, working class
or upper class, men or women as though that were the only thing
about us that mattered; the important thing is that as Christians we are one company of friends (A. Dale).

Life of the new man

Baptism is the beginning of the new life. The Christian life
is marked at the outset by a conversion: a turning from the sin
in the world to follow Christ in his death, and this must continue throughout life. Men must put off the old self and put on
the new self (Col. 3. 10). 'Created in Christ Jesus' (Eph. 2. 10)
for a life of good works they are to show the fact in their daily
life.

The renewal takes place by way of slow progressive sancti-
fication: 'our spiritual nature is being renewed every day'
(2 Cor. 4. 16). In so far as the old world of sin continues to
exist along with the new order of things inaugurated with Christ's
resurrection, the possibilities of sin exist in Christians along with
the new principle of grace. Consequently, they must ever be
careful. 'We've finished with the old ways of living with all
their nasty tricks. We're living in a new world — God's world —
and every day God will make us better skilled at living in it.
You've heard people talking like this, haven't you?: "My
country — right or wrong", "our religion's the right religion;
other religions are just superstition", "We're civilized; they're

wogs", "Some people are born slaves; they'll always be slaves".
We don't talk like that any more. We stand — always and
everywhere — for all that Jesus stood for' (Col. 3. 9-11. A.
Dale version).

The new man in the new world

Through the Christian, the new man, the work of renewal is
extended to the entire universe; Christ has reconciled all things
both on earth and in heaven with God (Col. 1. 20) and all
creation awaits redemption (Rom. 8. 19).

We may not isolate man from the world in which he lives and
works. This world of ours is already being transformed and will
find its fulfilment at the conclusion of history. In the meantime
Christians plan and strive for a better world. They do this not
under the illusion of a utopia within history, but because
material and social conditions must be such that man can fulfil
his task and live truly as God's image.

The question may well be asked why we are to strive for
progress when we know that the golden age can never be
achieved by human efforts and final fulfilment comes only as a
gift from God and beyond history. The better world for which
we are working will always remain limited and imperfect. Why
then must we strive for a perfect world? One can suggest a
satisfactory answer. On the one hand, human progress in this
world of ours is a partial anticipation of the final fulfilment for
which we are destined. It gives us a foretaste of the ultimate goal
of the history of salvation. It encourages us in the efforts we make
towards improving the world. On the other hand, our efforts
are accompanied with disappointments, failures, fatigue and
suffering. This aspect makes us realize the infinite distance
between us and our final destiny and the impossibility of reaching
it by our own efforts. Only God can give the ultimate goal, which
is eternal life, with all restrictions of time and space abolished.
So our human life is at once both a striving and a waiting for
God. We live in confidence of final success, because of our faith
in Jesus Christ. In Jesus Christ God accepted our human
situation, identified himself with us, lived through our sufferings
and hopes, and he rose to the beginning of the new world; and

through Jesus Christ our own life begins to be transformed and move towards its consummation in the glory of the eternal Father.

In the classroom

A series of lessons could be taken on the theme of this article with adolescents by discussing with them the following questions:

What is history?

Is history cyclic, i.e. with the same things happening over and over again? If so, have we any control over it?

Is history a kind of progression? If so, have we any control over it?

Can you point to any sort of evolution in the last thirty years?

Are we passive in the process of evolution?

Can we actively work for change?

Is change always good? Why or why not?

What is progress?

Do we have to go where science is able to take us — abandon individuality and self-control in the name of scientific progress?

How do you envisage a brave new world? (computerized society? death by pollution? love and justice?)

Have we a responsibility for bringing about a new world?

How can we ourselves work for a better world?

How is Christ the new man?

What is the new life he gives?

What is the new world he makes?

What does it mean to say Christ is in us and we are in Christ?

How do we work with Christ to build the new world?

What will be the 'new heaven and new earth' promised in scripture?

T. LYNCH

The problem of God

The most basic question facing Christians today is the problem of God. In one sense, for the intellectual Christian who distinguishes with M. Gabriel Marcel problem and mystery, God is not a problem; he is the only reality that is not a problem, since he is the only reality that is totally self-explanatory. But in another sense for all who are concerned to understand the historic Christian faith in a secular age God is certainly a problem. The majority of Englishmen, uninterested in religion, question the need for God. God is reckoned to be an outmoded idea that is intellectually superfluous, emotionally dispensable and morally intolerable. Surely, confronted with this secularistic outlook Christian theologians must see that their central problem is to establish the reality of God, not so much *whether* he is as *what* and *how* he is.

Turning to ourselves as committed Christians we find ourselves obliged to ask: how are we to think and speak intelligently of God? We have our own God-problem. We are people of our own time, sharing the same culture as the multitude of agnostics in our midst. We experience as difficulties those questionings which have led many of our contemporaries to abandon belief in God. We find it increasingly difficult to accept the old-style natural theology which employs a discarded world-view and a discredited metaphysical method. We are no longer satisfied with the sole appeal to a special revelation to the people of the Bible, because, if God wills the salvation of all men at all times, we expect a more universal self-disclosure of God than that found in scripture. Consequently, as Christians with the responsibility of proclaiming the good news of the living God, we experience the need to re-think the age-old statements of the Church and to speak of God in the language and concepts of modern people who have been brought up in a scientific mentality and who think (wrongly, we consider) that the scientific method is the sole means for obtaining knowledge.

Confusion of mind

The endless debates about God in recent years have left ordinary Christians more confused than ever, and in particular they have left teachers more puzzled how they are to think and speak of God in the presence of their students. The 'new theologians' have invited us to cast out false notions, but very few have done anything in the way of helping us positively to form a better concept. In fact, this writer is personally convinced that some of the radical theologians are making confusion worse confounded. They make the unwarrantable assumption that all metaphysics is to be dismissed. If one particular metaphysical theory happens to be discredited at the moment, it does not follow that all metaphysics can be rejected. The fundamental questions about the nature of reality are as open to philosophical enquiry as ever they were.

Our complaint is not directed to all modern theologians. A few of them are feeling their way to a new expression of our understanding of God. They are trying to discover the reality of God by an examination of human experience and they discern in that experience moments of divine transcendence that allow us to speak about God in terms of human possibilities.

It must not be forgotten that some confusion, or rather some obscurity, will always persist in the writings of even the best theologians, since they are grappling with the most difficult subject the mind of man can work upon, the incomprehensible God.

Godlessness

We frequently read and hear of the growing atheism of the modern world; perhaps it would be more accurate to speak of godlessness. Atheism suggests an explicit reflective denial of God. That there are true atheists or that they have strong arguments I do not deny, but I think they are relatively few in number. I am inclined to agree with John Baillie who maintains that many of the so-called atheists deny God 'with the top of their minds' but believe in him 'at the bottom of their hearts' (*Our Knowledge of God*, pp. 47-61). But godless-ness, or the rejection of God, is less intellectual; it concerns rather the choice of a style of life in which God is left out of account. This banishing of God from one's life is becoming more widespread.

The reasons for this godlessness need not be sought here; a number of them are presented in *The Church in the Modern World*, 19-21. It is the fact which concerns us. Many people have dispensed with God. He is absent from their lives, and the absence does not in the least disturb them, since they feel con-fident that they can get along quite well without him. Belief in God, it is thought, may have been reasonable and necessary in earlier pre-scientific days when he was seen as the meeter of needs and the solver of problems, but nowadays men have learned to take matters into their own hands and to be responsi-ble for their own history. They can exclude any supernatural agency at work in the world.

This godlessness is not confined to sophisticated adults; it exists among the pupils in our schools. These young people are influenced by the times in which they live and the grown-ups by whom they are surrounded.

Christian educators are expected to counter this godlessness. We do this best, not by refuting it directly or frequently talking about it, but by our own spirit of faith which will be detected by the pupils. By our way of thinking and speaking we make God known as a big Fact we are always meeting; we communi-cate the conviction that the world is really unintelligible without God and that there is no satisfactory explanation of man himself without the fact of God. Then, since one very common cause of godlessness is the fact that people entertain false ideas of the true God and have turned away from what is really a caricature of him, an urgent requirement is that the educator should present true notions of who God is and what he is like. But above all, the living witness of our own sincere belief in God, shown in the way we live and behave, by which is meant not only religious observances but more especially care and concern for our fellows, is the strong argument for the reality of God. This living witness causes us to be a sign in the world of the God we have met and known in Jesus Christ.

A rational foundation for belief

We know God only by faith. But our belief in God ought to stand up to rational investigation. Most of our teenagers begin to question what they have been brought up to believe; it is a good thing that they should be critical in this way, since without some rational foundations for their beliefs, their faith will hardly survive the secularist spirit of the modern world.

These young people unaccustomed to philosophy, are perhaps best helped by some *informal* reasoning which supports their religious belief. Newman was probably correct in holding that the easiest and commonest informal reasoning is through conscience and the moral law. Teachers might make use of this argument, which is to be found in manuals. A good book on the subject is *The Moral Argument for Christian Theism* by H. Power.

This informal reasoning is not always enough; more thoughtful students will want some conscious formal reasoning, by which is meant some rational arguments pointing to the reality of God. We could, then, engage upon the arguments which have been used for the existence of God, preferably following the more modern re-statements of the traditional 'five ways'.

We must acknowledge that the arguments do not 'prove' God's existence; their value lies in assuring those who believe that their belief has a sound basis in reason. It should be realized that they fall into place and have some importance only *after* one has had some teaching about what God is.

God talk

God has become irrelevant to many people because much of our religious language is mediaeval and conceals the reality we want to point to in God. Even the word 'God' has become elusive; so much confusion has grown around it that some writers go so far as to say that the word is now dead, and should not be used. They exaggerate. But to test the confusion even among firm believers I invite you to examine yourself and notice how easily you use the word God with a different meaning in different contexts and how with equal ease you slip from one meaning to another in the same conversation without making the fact clear. At one moment you mean the God of philosophers, at another God the Father and at another the Christian triune God. Or take any of those words describing God which we were taught from childhood days: infinite, eternal, omnipotent, omniscient, omnipresent. Each one of them has to be understood with a meaning different from the ordinary meaning. This is confusing to adults as well as to young people. However, a word of warning: having recognized the inadequacy of our Christian vocabulary it would be arrogance on our part to find fault with ordinary older Christians who want to go on using the old language in their prayers and conversation.

Some of our words which were once assets at the time of early controversies, substance, person, nature, and so on, are now liabilities when we try to communicate the doctrine of God. Much of our language, assuming a static vertical world view, fails to register nowadays and gives rise to misconceptions in the minds of the people to whom we are talking. Consequently, in order to speak intelligibly of God we must meet our contemporaries where they are and use a language they understand. Nevertheless, in giving preference to language and concepts that are current today, depth, concern, encounter, relationships, and so on, we must be on our guard against diluting the truth or inventing a new God in an excessive desire to be contemporary. Above all, we must make certain that the God we speak about is the same God as the God of the Bible and of Christian tradition.

Thus both the Bible and Christian tradition recognize that God is not simply radically different from other beings but that he is not *a* being at all along with or over against the universe. He is so utterly different that we can speak of him only in symbols and analogies, 'creator', 'revealer', 'personal', 'transcendent', 'of another order', 'on another level' and the like. We are justified in speaking in this oblique way provided that we remind ourselves — which we do not — that it *is* symbolic language. The symbol 'creator', for example, expresses his relationship to the world and the fact that all things are ultimately dependent on God. The symbol 'revealer' refers to the fact that God relates himself to men and makes himself known.

No break with tradition

There seems to be among some writers a desire to ignore what the past has taught us about God. They insinuate that the abstract God of metaphysical theology is irrelevant and that the personal God of the Bible is incredible. All this, they think, must be left aside and a fresh approach needs to be made to the whole question of God. These writers are brash to say the least; they would make God change with every changing fashion of thought. I agree that each generation must think out its idea of God from the newness of its own situation and that mere repetition of inherited formulas would not lead to any real present-day understanding. But we cannot afford to ignore the traditional doctrine of God and the serious thinking of our predecessors. There can be no question of abandoning the God spoken of in the Bible and the creeds. The ever-living God is the same God throughout history, and we are nourished from past thinking. Our task is to build upon the genuine Christian tradition our own conception of God making use of whatever new insights our present knowledge of man and the world may be giving us. Admittedly, this involves a tension between fidelity to the past (creeds, doctrinal propositions, liturgies) and the demands of a present response of faith. But the tension has to be lived with under the power of the Spirit.

The event of Christ

Christians believe that whilst God reveals himself in numerous ways to men, he reveals himself fully in Christ. Jesus Christ 'is the fullness of all revelation' (DV). We need to understand this statement correctly, since many good Christians do not; they argue to themselves: Jesus Christ is God; therefore he is the full revelation of God. By this over-simplification they completely ignore the consequences of the Incarnation!

Jesus of Nazareth was a first century Jew who was conscious of having a mission in life to proclaim the imminence of God's kingly rule. Being as human as any of us he had to grow like the rest of us in knowledge of himself, of his relationship to other people and to God. God spoke to Jesus as he speaks to all men, namely in his conscious human experience. As revelation is not revelation unless some one hears God's word and responds to it, Jesus grew in the knowledge of God because he listened carefully to the word of God, sought for it and responded always with love and faithfulness. This growth was not a painless effortless receiving of light from God; from the gospels we gather that Jesus endured the searchings and uncertainties that we experience in finding the will of God. Like men before and after him he must have felt some hesitation when some conviction of his seemed a personal opinion or contrary to the orthodox teaching of the religious leaders. He was so attentive to the word of God and so faithful in his response that he developed an exceptional understanding of God's revelation, and God was able to reveal himself both to and in the man Jesus in a unique manner. By the unique manner of God's self-revelation we mean that God was personally present for us in the man Jesus, in whom his self-revelation throughout previous ages by actions and words reached its highest point and clearest meaning. The attitudes and actions of Jesus were those of God.

God's word is received in a community. Jesus was a member of the Jewish community. What the gospels report of his language, his religion, his way of thinking show that he was very much a man of his own time and place. He was well acquainted with the traditions of his race, and was recognized by some of the people as an authentic prophet and taken by others to be a false prophet. Like the prophets of old who said something new he was welcomed and rejected. In the end he suffered the fate of many an earlier prophet: he was persecuted and put to death.

The death on the cross was the supreme revelation of God's love for men and the supreme response of love on the part of Jesus on behalf of mankind.

By his death and resurrection Jesus passed to a new life. With his exaltation he came to possess the fullness of revelation; for the Holy Spirit could now completely transform him, and he became totally open to God in a far more perfect manner than was possible when he was limited by time and space. He received the full revelation of God as his humanity entered into the fullness of the Godhead. From the resurrection onwards the fullness of divine revelation resides in the consciousness of Jesus Christ, or in other words, in Jesus Christ we have the full revela-

tion of God. God has revealed to the risen Christ everything
he has to say and has nothing more to add. The risen Christ
is alive today on earth. He remains present in his Body, the
Church. He shares his knowledge of the Father with the members
of his Body. So God is in Christ continuing to reveal himself in
Christ's Body, which is the community of Christians.

The consciousness of the living Christ is an evolving
consciousness, not in the sense that anything new is added to
the once-for-all given revelation in the Christ-Event, but in the
sense that as the community-Body of Christ moves through the
varying circumstances of history Christ mediates revelation in
the context of these changing conditions and will do so until the
Body reaches due completion at the end of time. The evolution
we speak of is something like the growth of a human person. The
person at the age of forty has characteristics that are different
from those he had at the age of four, but he is just the same
person.

Son and Word

It was after the resurrection, when the first disciples had
deeply reflected upon the earthly career and resurrection of their
master, that they were able to interpret the uniqueness of Jesus.
Before the resurrection they had seen that the Jesus of Nazareth
with whom they had walked and lived enjoyed a unique relationship with God. This came out in his words, attitudes, actions
and his whole character. After the resurrection they came to a
fuller understanding in faith, and they described his uniqueness
by saying that Jesus was the Son of God and Word of God.

The gospel narratives give evidence that Jesus spoke of God
as being his Father in a unique way, making a distinction
between 'my Father' and 'your Father'. But in what did his
sonship consist? The early Christians seem at first to have used
the title 'the Son of God' to denote Jesus' unique relationship
with God the Father in love and obedience, but fairly soon they
came to a deeper understanding of its significance as denoting
divinity in him: Jesus is divine as the Father is divine. This
being so, Jesus as Son could make known the Father, and to see
Jesus was to see the Father.

St John calls Jesus the Word of God. He has borrowed this term from early Jewish writings and current Greek philosophic speculation. The Israelites understood God's Word to be pre-existent with God, essentially divine, creator of all that exists, the source of light and life. The Word of God fully expresses God. John tells us that this Word of God became flesh in the person of Jesus Christ, who is thus the embodiment in human terms of what God is. Jesus Christ, therefore, makes God known in a human way.

Catechetical conclusions

The catechist will never forget that the truest and most concrete knowledge of God comes to us through Jesus Christ. Jesus Christ is God for us. Without him we would not really know God. And the more we come to know Jesus in whom God lives a truly human life, the better we come to know God. If anyone says he feels the absence of God far more than his presence, we can advise him to get to know Jesus Christ and he will assuredly find God in our midst.

When we recognize that God is in Jesus Christ (2 Cor. 5. 19) we shall help students to see God through Christ. And if they want to know how they stand in relation to God, they may be told to ask themselves how they stand in relation to Jesus Christ, the one way to the Father.

Since God speaks and acts through men, especially the man Jesus Christ, we shall encourage students to be more attentive in listening to men and in loving them; moreover, they should be led to look more deeply into human existence, to examine earthly experiences and occupations, rather than to speculate about some non-existent 'other world'. They should learn to recognize the presence and action of Christ in their own personal experience, realizing that at the core of each one's search for truth and fuller life is Jesus Christ, the truth and the life.

F. SOMERVILLE

G

The reality of God

We cannot prove the reality of God by syllogisms. What in our youth used to be called proofs are at best arguments to show that it is possible that God exists. These traditional arguments are at the moment out of favour, because they involve a metaphysical way of thinking that is now being radically questioned. Can we, then, provide arguments which give rational support to our Christian belief in God? [1]

Attempts at new ways

The answer is Yes. At the present day there are, in Anglo-Saxon countries, three major types of philosophy: process philosophy, existentialism and logical empiricism. Christian theologians are making use of the insights and categories of these current philosophies in order to speak of God in terms intelligible to men of our times who refuse to accept the traditional arguments.

As we cannot go into each of these here, I shall simply indicate some works which the interested reader might like to read. Thus the process philosophies which lay main stress on becoming, and so take seriously the notions of time and development, in contrast to the old philosophies that think of the real in terms of timeless unchanging substance, have won the attention of Christian theologians like Norman W. Pittenger (*God in Process; Process Thought and Christian Faith*) and Schubert M. Ogden (*The Reality of God*). These 'process theologians', starting from the world we experience in all its concreteness and variety, point to a God who does not dwell in timeless perfection apart from this world (as in scholastic theology) but is involved in

---

[1] It is well to remember that our knowledge of God does not really come from ourselves, but is a gift from God. We know him because he reveals himself, not because of our own effort to discover him. It is true that we can rightly speak of man's innate quest for God, but God has already met man and begun to make himself known by provoking that quest.

mutual action and passion with the world yet at the same time transcending it.

The existential philosophers have given rise to two groups of Christian existential theologians. One group (for example, Bultmann in his *Jesus Christ and Mythology*, and F. Gogarten in *Demythologizing and History*) explores contemporary man's secular self-understanding and finds in it areas that are open to God's action. But it must be confessed that the idea of God among these authors is very obscure indeed. The other group, represented by P. Tillich (*Systematic Theology, Vol.* 1) and to some extent John A. Robinson (*Exploration into God*) have adopted what might be called an existential-ontological theism. They start from man's self-understanding, and they find him to be concerned with the question of being, and with the Being that is present and manifest in the beings that constitute the world. In so far as man experiences this Being as holy, then he rightly calls it God.

Perhaps the most notable Christian theologian today, who has employed thought-forms drawn from the logical empiricists, is Dr Ian Ramsey, Bishop of Durham (*Religious Language; Models and Mystery*). He seeks to show that if we do not understand empiricism in too narrow a sense, we can acknowledge that our experience of certain situations has a depth to it which he characterizes in terms of 'discernment and commitment'. The combination of these two is characteristic of every religious conversion.

These laudable attempts of Christian thinkers to talk the language of the secular world show to modern man that he is not the self-sufficient person he is sometimes represented to be, and that he can reach a true self-understanding only if there is opened up for him the reality of God. At the same time none of the new theologies has yet been sufficiently worked out to command a general consensus.

All this searching and reasoning we have just noted is taking place at an academic level. But is there any argument for the reality of God which would satisfy the minds of plain Christians, the mass of those who are not specialized in theology? I think that anyone who has reached a certain maturity can come to an awareness and conviction of God's presence from the experience of human love.

Preliminary remarks

We should enquire into what we know from experience, the only access to genuine knowledge. Today people are suspicious, rightly or wrongly, of some preconceived system of thought, such as the supernaturalistic theism of classical metaphysics; they rely rather on the logic of experience. For them the norm of truth is human experience. They ask: is the assertion logically self-consistent and warranted by common experience? This being so we had better be agreed on what is meant by experience. Brother Gabriel Moran has defined it as the totality of human interaction with the environment. Another writer says that 'experience is not only the actual facing of situations, events and persons, it includes the knowledge gathered from the practical dealings with them'. From this it must be noted that experience is more than the passive acceptance of persons and things through the senses. Experience is the *product* of a meeting or encounter between a person who accepts, responds to and interprets the encounter and the persons or things encountered. Here it should be pointed out that only men can have experience in the sense given, because only men respond to, interpret and express their experience; and that the original encounter with the person or thing is only the beginning of experience. If the initial encounter is deemed worthwhile it will be protracted and become more or less permanent.

Another preliminary remark needs to be made. A characteristic mark of the present generation is the deepened interest in the human person and a more profound appreciation of persons. We seem to recognize much more fully than previous ages the uniqueness and transcendent value of each person.

To become truly human is to be a person. We need other selves for our own selfhood. We become personal and grow in personality in response to persons. Is not this the reason why educationists and young people especially attach great importance to human relationships?

And even apart from thoughts of human development most people today in our 'global village' feel involved with their fellowmen. With the mass media entering our homes we cannot be or feel unconcerned for our neighbours in Vietnam or

Northern Ireland. A rumour of cholera in Spain leads Englishmen to take precautions; a political disturbance in the Middle
East brings all Europe to military alert.

The experience of love

Those who have experienced true human love, for example
of a man for a woman, or of a friend for a friend, often experience
a presence and a demand in their relationship which are sometimes startling and usually too deep to put into words. It is
an overwhelming experience. What is this presence? What is
this demand? They can hardly analyse it, but it is something
very real, as real as their deep love. They feel both attraction
and awe, of what we might almost call the numinous. They sense
a dimension of love which is somehow deeper than the face-value
of their loving experiences. They feel the presence of mystery in
true human love. They have an awareness of some reality here
that cannot be explained by any scientific explanation; and this
reality must be personal because it is there in the depths of the
human person.

Moreover, the human love of the man and woman very often
points beyond their present loving relationship to some future
fulfilment which seems far richer than anything so far attained.
They have intimations of a perfection of love.

These various features of our experience of deep human
love point to some ultimate personal reality underlying all our
loving. It may be called Love, with a capital letter. Christians
call it God.

When we speak in this way we proclaim the reality of God
in a relevant way to people of our day without diluting or
distorting any truth of the Christian faith. God, being unseen
and spirit, cannot disclose himself immediately, but does so
through a created medium. He does so especially in people and
personal relationships, of which I have taken a special example.
Moreover, we hold that God has not disclosed himself only to the
Israelites and to Christians, but that he makes himself known to
all men, whether they are religious-minded or not. For the
experience of deep human love is open to all men of any creed
or none; it is a universal disclosure of God. Again, Christians

speak of God as Love and as personal; if he is to be experienced anywhere, it will surely be above all in persons and in personal love, as has been suggested in this description and interpretation of true human love.

This argument (perhaps intuition would be a better term to use) does not prove the *reality* of God. It might not satisfy an unbeliever; but it does put forward a claim that he must take seriously; for he will hardly deny the mystery in true human love. He is confronted with a live option that cannot be lightly dismissed. However, the main concern here is, as has been said, to supply a supporting scaffolding for faith, to help Christians satisfy to their own minds the reasonableness of their belief in God. And I think that the line suggested is particularly appropriate and significant to the present generation.

Perhaps I ought to give reasons for this statement. Christians today are moving away from understanding God's transcendence as God dwelling far away in some upper region and directing our lives from a distance. All of them have always agreed that he is somehow active in the world, but now almost all sense that he must be present within the world.

Christians today are very conscious of living in a totally involved world where what one person does affects all the rest. We are 'all in it together'. If God is for real, then he must be involved. They would prefer to do without a God who is not concerned with all the persons of the world.

Personalism is very strong today. The old cosmological and ontological arguments of natural theology do not appeal to men and women living in a personalistic universe. They are seeking the meaning of life, as human beings have always done throughout the centuries, which means they are seeking some ultimate reality, but they feel that ultimate reality must be personal rather than a first cause, a prime mover or a necessary being. They are on the way to a new natural theology.

In maintaining that God is experienced at the heart of human love in the depths of the human person, we meet the articulate or inarticulate questionings of our contemporaries. For God is seen to be very much in this world, wherever there is true love; he is involved in all human relationships which should manifest love; and he is personal because love is personal.

The God of Jesus

We can now turn to a quite different way for coming to have adequate grounds for believing in the reality of God. Take the man Jesus of Nazareth and study carefully his consciousness of God. Even a cursory reading of the four gospels shows that his whole life, as far as we know it, was dominated by his consciousness of his heavenly Father. The evangelists bring this out in a score of ways. They make his first recorded saying, as a boy of twelve, one that affirms he was aware of a close relationship with the Father: 'Did you not know that I must be in my Father's house?' (Lk 2. 49). At the beginning of his public career he experienced being called as a Son by his Father to carry out a commission (Mk 1. 49). Jesus spent his time teaching; all his teaching was wholly about God, to make God as real to his hearers as he was to himself. Jesus went about healing people; all these healings were done in the name of God; they were manifestations of what would be universal when God's rule was everywhere established. During the passion Jesus was conscious that he was doing his Father's will. Finally, his dying words showed that his mind was turned towards God: 'Father, into thy hands I commit my spirit' (Lk 23. 46). God was as real to Jesus as was Mary, Peter, James and John.

Having studied Jesus from this point of view, his consciousness of God, we may now ask ourselves whether it was reasonable for Jesus to believe in the reality of God on the basis of his own experience. The immediate answer we might give is Yes. But such an answer does not prove that what he believed is true. A man can be under a compelling delusion as well as under a compelling recognition of truth. So we have to ask the further question: do we think the man Jesus of Nazareth was a victim of delusion or a sane individual. Again, we look at the gospels to find an answer. The gospels do not give an answer; each one of us must decide his own answer, and this answer will be decided by each one's individual response to the person of Jesus. If I conclude that he was sane, I shall also conclude that he was right in his compelling belief. If I conclude he was insane, I shall not follow him in his delusion.

This is not the end of the reflection. We have to make up our minds about the conviction of Jesus within a wider back-

ground. What is our own understanding of the universe? Do
we think it *possible* that a Creator God exists? When we reflect
upon the universe we come to learn a lot of things about it:
what things are, the interrelation of things and how they function.
With the help of physics, chemistry, astronomy and other
sciences we can go on increasing our knowledge of the 'how'
of things and of the universe. But we still remain baffled by the
'why': why should there be anything at all? why is there a
universe at all? This question does not force us to answer that
there must be a Creator. The fact that I exist, that things exist,
that the universe exists does not *prove* that God exists as a first
cause. But it does present us with the possibility that God exists.

It is within this wider background situation that we come
back to the person of Jesus and the question of whether he was
sane or a man living under a delusion.

Suppose we cannot help but be convinced that Jesus was
sane and that we feel compelled to affirm all that he stands for,
that his life and teaching are eminently human. We then ask:
is it reasonable *for me* to believe in God? If Jesus, who was so
very conscious of the reality of God in his life, was reasonable
in his believing in God, am I, on my lower level of religious
experience, also reasonable in believing in God? Does his
experience of living in the presence of God find some echo in
my own experience? Does his teaching about the heavenly
Father become credible to me? If so, then my belief in the reality
of God is as rational as I am.

Notice that this way of thinking is based upon the religious
experience of Jesus and our own religious experience. For
Christians it has an impelling character and helps to give a
rational basis for their belief. For anyone who does not share
that religious experience of the presence of God, it cannot be
expected to carry any weight; such a person may be impressed
by reading the gospels, but he cannot be expected to believe in
God on the basis of Jesus's words; he must be a religious man
himself possessing some religious experience. The argument
claims to do nothing more than assure believers that their belief
has a sound basis in reason.

T. LYNCH

Where is God?

This sounds an innocent and reasonable question. Every child has asked it at some time. Every Christian adult asks it and answers it perhaps more with the imagination than with reason. Yet imagination is notoriously misleading. For many centuries most Christians thought that God was up in heaven, somewhere above the clouds. The Copernican revolution squashed that idea. So they gradually moved over to the pictorial image of God living somewhere outside the universe beyond space. Incidentally, since he was so very far away whether spatially or metaphysically, many men felt they had no use for such a remote God and let him drop out of mind. Good Catholics, however, at the same time clung to the catechism answer. 'God is everywhere', and still using imagination more than reason, would concede, if pressed, that God is up a tree, in the top drawer of the dressing table, in their pocket. Surely, some consideration of the presence of God is called for.

The statement 'God is nowhere' is just as true as the statement 'God is everywhere'. Both answers can be correctly given to our question. This sounds absurd. But the reason is that the question itself, which appears reasonable, cannot be legitimately asked. The word 'where' expects an answer involving location in space and time, it expects a 'here' or 'there'. Moreover, that same word supposes you are talking about some object whose whereabouts you are seeking. But God, who is Spirit and wholly Other than the world, cannot be placed in space or time. Properly speaking, he is neither inside nor outside the world. Nor is God an object or even like an object; for in his total otherness he cannot be one more object (however exalted) among or over against other objects we know and can examine. Consequently, since the question presupposes notions of time, space and object, which cannot be applied to God, it cannot legitimately be asked.

God is nowhere

Nevertheless, although the question cannot be asked, it must be answered. The first correct answer is: God is nowhere.

God is not up in the heavens above or down in the waters beneath the earth. He is not out there in some outer space beyond this world. He is neither here nor there inside this world. To be somewhere is to be here and not there, or there and not here; if a thing is here it is absent from there and vice versa. When my pencil is lying on the table it is not in my pocket. In other words, to be somewhere is to be related to other spatial things. Persons and things in the world are spatially related to each other, and it is this spatial relatedness which places them somewhere.

But God, the wholly Other, is not an object alongside the world; so he is not spatially related to anyone or anything. That is why he is not in space at all. God is, in the spatial sense, nowhere. The Soviet astronaut who announced that he did not find God 'up there' was indulging in a cheap sneer. The atheistic scientist who says that if God exists science will discover him is making a very unscientific statement, because the spatial absence of God means that he is unobservable and undetectable by any method of science.

God is everywhere

Approaching the same question, again in line with the true Christian tradition, we may give the answer that God is everywhere.

God is Creator. He makes things to be. The pencil, lying on my table, exists. I exist. Workmen modifying various materials made the pencil. They are responsible for the becoming of the pencil from wood, lead and paint, but not for its being. My parents came together in the marriage act and made me; they are responsible for my becoming their son, but not for my being. God and the workmen work together, without rivalry, to make the pencil; God and parents work together to make the child. The workmen and parents put the materials together and produce the finished article. God lets the makers and the materials to be, to exist. God's creative activity causes things to be and continue to be. Wherever there is anything at all, there is God's creative activity, letting it to be. Therefore, wherever anything exists, there is God in his creative activity. In a word, God is creatively everywhere.

The reader will recognize here the doctrine of creation. God as Creator continually gives being to his creatures. 'In him all things live, move and have their being'. He is present to the world and at the heart of all that exists, without interfering with the autonomy proper to the world, an autonomy which the Creator has granted to the world. The hidden God is not distant or absent; he is always near.

God present in Jesus Christ

Christians also say that God is in Jesus Christ. The doctrine of the Incarnation tells of the presence and manifestation of God. St John summed up the matter briefly: 'The Word became flesh and dwelt among us . . . we have beheld his glory'. The 'Word' is a biblical term denoting the creative, life-giving God in his outward expression. 'Flesh' is also a biblical term denoting what is creaturely, frail, mortal, human. What has happened, then, is that the creative Word has taken on himself the condition of man in its entirety. He has done so in the person of the man called Jesus of Nazareth. Jesus is as fully and genuinely human as you or I and at the same time the embodiment of God's personal action in human history. The human actions and attitudes of Jesus are at the same time the actions and attitudes of God. At the centre of Christian belief is the fact that God is present and manifest in Jesus Christ, the Incarnate Word.

God present in the Church

No man is an island. Each one of us is related to others, to our families, to various communities of which we are members, and ultimately to the whole of humankind. Being human implies, among other things, being-with other persons. The risen Jesus, still living in the world today, cannot be separated from the community of those men and women who have joined themselves to him and are animated by his Spirit. We call this community his body or the Church. The Church is the body of Christ in the world. We must affirm, then, following upon what we have seen in the previous paragraph, that God is present and manifest in the Church, apart from which Christ has no independent existence.

The Church, as we see it in the world, is a fully human

society that can carry on only through institutional structures. Many of its institutions and structures are at present under attack as being obsolete, oppressive, useless or harmful, but not even the severest critic would imagine for a moment that the Church could exist without some institutions and structures. The necessity of these earthly things goes to show the insufficiently recognized truth that God becomes present and manifest through the medium of things that are very human.

God present in men

A few generations ago men could experience the presence of God in beauties of nature such as the delicacy of flowers, the grandeur of mountains and so on. But today whilst that witness need not be excluded, it is not so direct and telling, since nature has become the profane object of scientific research. We do better perhaps to turn to the world of men, and, in this strongly personalist age in which we live, reflect upon our experiences with and of other people.

When a reflective person, Christian or not, looks beneath the surface and tries to discover what are man's deepest concerns he finds them to be loving personal relationships. He becomes convinced that fully personal love, self-giving and demanding by its very nature, is of ultimate concern in human life. His own experience of it within the family and with friends, together with the known experiences of others, leads him to perceive or sense a mysterious dimension of human life. The experience of love points beyond itself to some reality which underlies all our deepest relationships and all our living. It is present to us and deep within us. What is it?

The Christian who makes these reflections will reply with a 'he', not 'it'. He brings to his thinking certain other relevant considerations. Centuries ago the experience of God's people led them to the conviction of a loving personal God. The coming of Christ and two thousand years of further experience have confirmed the conviction that 'God is love'. As Creator he is present to all his creatures, creatively initiating and freshly sustaining all that exists. But we have very good reasons to believe that he is especially present to and in human beings. First, he made man in his own image. This means that despite the distinction between Creator and creature, there is a real affinity between man and God. Man has received freedom, reason, the power to love, and, above all, the power to love his Creator, and therefore to have fellowship with God. God is present in every man to share his love and receive a return of love. Secondly and more important, in Jesus Christ God and man are one. By becoming present in Jesus the Christ, God has shown himself to be Emmanuel, which means 'God with us', leading us through the complexity of human experience to the fullness of life in the age to come. In becoming man God gave himself utterly to us in the total self-giving love which marked Jesus's life. By the Incarnation God took on himself the entire experience of existence as man, so much so that one can say that God has become 'humanized' in all mankind, not in Christians only, but in all men. God, who is love, is present here and now as love in everyone.

Love has many countenances. Wherever a good act is performed, there is God. All goodness derives from God. Wherever truth is spoken, there is God. Wherever beauty is admired, there is God. Wherever there is concern for others, compassion, forgiveness, mercy, work for peace, we perceive the activity of God. We do not say that the love and goodness that is found in every man is God; for to say that God is love does not allow us to say that love is God. God can never be made a predicate.

The above considerations can be put to pastoral use by teachers with their students and by priests with their congregations. God is not someone who lives away in a world of his own. He is present in this world involved in our everyday lives. We meet him whenever we enter into loving relationships with our fellow human beings. Since he is utter goodness we experience him as deep within and sustaining the love we show to others and the love they show to us. It is in these human encounters that God is to be found.

Transcendence and immanence

What we have been saying in this article is closely bound up with what the theologians since the early centuries have called God's transcendence and immanence, two Greek concepts which are drawn from the scriptures where they are expressed in a less abstract language.

To say God is transcendent means that God is qualitatively different from all else that we can think of, that he surpasses all creation, is distinct from it, and is far beyond anything our concepts can grasp. The Bible means the same when it speaks of God's sovereignty or his holiness.

To say that God is immanent means that God is present in all that exists, sustaining in being all that exists. St Paul expresses this idea when he says that 'in him (God) we live and move and have our being'.

In any thinking about God it is vitally important to keep in mind that God is both transcendent and immanent, or, better still, transcendently immanent, since this helps us to avoid a dualist manner of speaking of God. It is vitally important to keep these two ideas together because every single mistake that people make about what God is comes from forgetting or under-estimating one of these two. The two must be kept together if we wish to avoid a false or distorted view of God. Thus, those people who concentrate their attention on God's transcendence imagine him to be totally distinct and separate from the world. They come to imagine him as having no concern for what goes on in the world. In the field of religious attitudes these people tend to find God to be some first principle with whom one cannot be in warm relation. On the other hand, those who concentrate exclusively on God's immanence, his presence in and to created things confuse him with the world and fall into some form of pantheism.

Some theologians today criticize traditional teaching for laying too much stress on God's transcendence, making him distinct from us, to the neglect of his nearness to us. They exaggerate the neglect of God's immanence; for this idea is contained in many of our prayers and hymns, St Patrick's Breastplate for instance. Yet they do right in wanting to make Christians more aware of God's presence in the world working with men to improve it and bring it to completion.

God, then, is transcendently immanent in the world. His transcendence or otherness or sovereignty does not prevent him from being immanent in creatures. He does not come down from above, because he is already here in our midst and closer to us than our breathing.

J. Low

Gospel truth

The gospels are our primary source for studying the person and work of Jesus. It is, therefore, very important to understand what a gospel is, in particular its literary form. Yet most Catholics take an over-simple view of the gospels. At the level of implicit faith this does not make much difference, but at the level of explicit faith and of theology great difficulties arise; for once we grasp what the gospels really are, we find we have to change our ideas about nearly everything we used to think of the narratives concerning Jesus. Here lies perhaps the chief differentiation between teachers of the old school and teachers who are trying to bring the benefits of biblical renewal to their pupils.

The common simple view is that the four gospels are accounts of what Jesus said and did. They were written down by inspired writers for our information. They are God's word, and consequently free from error. Taken together they give a life of Jesus; their accounts complement each other. The evangelists have given accurate reports of what Jesus said and did, because the apostles and eye-witnesses would not have allowed them to misrepresent their Master.

How the gospels arose

However, this popular view cannot stand up to criticism, and it is now being revised. One has only to examine how the gospels arose to realize how mistaken it is. We have no less an authority than the Pontifical Biblical Commission to confirm this statement. In 1964 the Commission issued an important 'Instruction on the historical truth of the gospels'. In it the Commission distinguishes three stages in the gradual formation of our gospel records. It is important to realize that the four gospels were written thirty to seventy years after the events they relate. During the long interval between the actual events and the texts we read today many things happened which affected the final writing, and these factors must obviously be taken into account when considering the truth and reliability of the gospels.

The first stage was the ministry of Jesus in Palestine when

he preached his message following the ways of thinking and speaking of his own time.

The second stage, extending over many years, was the preaching and teaching of the apostles who had been commissioned by Jesus to carry on his work. The apostles began by *preaching* to non-Christians. They proclaimed the 'good news' of Jesus, the man in whom God had definitively entered human history for man's salvation. This Jesus is alive. This Jesus is the Lord. We have an example of their preaching in Peter's first sermon on the day of Pentecost (Acts 2). Not all the facts about Jesus' life were needed for this preaching; the apostles considered it sufficient to present the decisive facts necessary to invite and establish faith in the hearers. The passion, death and resurrection were judged the most important facts.

An obvious development soon took place. After the preaching was heard and accepted, the converts would want to know more about Jesus the Christ and the religious implications of his life witness for their own lives. Thus apostolic *teaching* followed upon apostolic preaching, which of course did not cease. The early Christians looked for more information about Jesus and for a legitimate understanding of his words and deeds. The still living eye-witnesses of Jesus recalled and interpreted events in his life and drew conclusions from them for living the Christian life in those days. In this way the initial preaching filled out into a more developed gospel tradition.

Naturally the early Christian teachers adopted various ways of speaking which suited their purpose and the needs of their hearers. This explains why the one gospel message came down in a variety of forms: 'catecheses, narratives, testimonies, hymns, doxologies, prayers and other literary forms of the kind which holy scripture and the people of that time were wont to employ' (Instruction of Pontifical Biblical Commission). Moreover, bits of the oral teaching would gradually be put into writing for the benefit of new local communities.

The third stage in the formation of the gospels was the writing of them by the evangelists. After a long interval (thirty to seventy years), during which the infant Church reflected on and recorded orally and in writing the things which Jesus said and did, the sacred authors, known as evangelists, made use of this great variety of accumulated material as their source to compile the four gospels. Only John among the evangelists was an eye-witness of Jesus. Assuming that the gospels were written by the men to whom they are ascribed, Mark was not one of the apostles; he was a disciple of Peter from whom he obtained much of his knowledge about Jesus; Luke was a convert of Paul; the gospel of Matthew, as we have it, is based on a previous version written in Aramaic, on Mark's gospel and on some other special sources. John's gospel is so heavily theologized that we cannot call it an eye-witness account in our sense of this term.

The evangelists were Christians writing for Christians, an in-group for the in-group. They gathered their materials from the varied oral traditions and small units of writings and compiled a record which reflected the beliefs of the early Church. This is important to note. They were not writing a history of Jesus. They were expressing the faith of the early Christian community in the risen Jesus, and to do so they drew upon incidents and sayings which genuinely referred back to the life of Jesus as the background and context. Being themselves firm believers they were qualified to interpret the significance of Jesus' actions and describe the reactions of Christian believers to the events narrated.

The evangelists felt free to arrange their material as they pleased. They were writing a faith document, not history. We expect historians to tell us as accurately as possible and in the right sequence when and where events took place and how they developed. The evangelists were not concerned about the exact sequence of events. Basing themselves on certain known facts related to Jesus they simply linked the episodes with vague phrases like 'at that time', 'then', 'next', 'a short time after', which do not indicate precise time or place. Moreover, they were not at all worried by minor divergences in relating an episode, for example whether it was one or two blind men at Jericho, whether it was on entering or on leaving there that the incident took place. Lots of such discrepancies are found in the gospels, but they do not matter, given the viewpoint of the evangelists: expression of the faith of the community. In the example just chosen, the central fact was that Jesus healed somebody.

The evangelists were not concerned with writing a biography of Jesus. They tell us quite a number of things about him, but

H

they do not give us a life of Jesus. And even some of the things we do know to have happened remain uncertain, the date of his birth and death for instance, the length of his public ministry, the number of visits to Jerusalem, the order of events in the last week. . . . Nevertheless, the evangelists do give us a valuable portrait of Jesus from which we can derive some insight into the richness of his person.

In handling their material the evangelists adapted it to the situation of their readers and to the purpose they themselves had in mind. They all used the traditions of the Christian community, but each one did so in his own way. Each one wrote according to his personal character and with a special aim, for special needs of Jewish or Gentile Christians.

The gospels are patently compilations. Within each we find words of Jesus, paraphrases of his sayings, echoes of the initial apostolic preaching, some form of pre-gospel teaching, interpretations of the early Church, reflections of the evangelist himself.

I have already stressed that the gospels were written many years after the events they narrate. This distance in time was bound to influence the manner of writing. If I sit down to write about some incident in my own childhood, I inevitably write as an adult and see it now through adult eyes; I almost certainly colour it to suit my present purposes. The gospels were written long after the resurrection. The writers knew the end of the story. When they narrated the events in Jesus' life they saw those events through the perspective of the resurrection, and this glorious outcome coloured all their writings.

Fact and interpretation

The conclusions of what we have been saying, following highly reputable scripture scholars, prove very disquieting to many teachers and liberating to others. Some find them disquieting, because they find they have to change so many ideas they had hitherto held. They also find there is not a single sentence in any of the four gospels which they do not have to read with new eyes. Those teachers who experience liberation find they can make the gospels much more intelligible and acceptable to their pupils. Let us summarize these conclusions which help us to know what a gospel is and how we are to understand 'gospel truth'.

The gospels are entirely human documents, and therefore no more free from historical error than any other ancient document. They are subject to criticism as any other literary work is. It is nonsense to suppose they are above criticism on the grounds that they are divinely inspired. The fact that it is often impossible to harmonize different accounts of the same incident proves that they cannot all be accurately reported.

The gospels do not give history as we understand it. The evangelists had other aims. A gospel does not claim to report accurately the deeds and sayings of Jesus nor to tell his life story. The problem of the historicity of the gospels in the way we used to formulate it is obsolete and irrelevant. The question is not: are the gospels historically reliable? As regards details, if some one asks: how did Jesus re-act in such or such a situation? the answer is: we do not always know; we only know how the evangelists presented him as re-acting. Did Jesus walk on the water? We do not know; we know the story told by the evangelist, but we do not know the precise facts behind the story. Very often whatever attempt we make to reconstruct what actually happened will only be guess work. Did Jesus really say: Be perfect as your heavenly Father is perfect? We do not know; we know the evangelists reported him as saying many things. Some of the sayings do have an authentic ring and may well be genuine quotations, but we cannot expect all his very words to survive in people's memories verbatim for so many years before the writing of the gospels; it is much more likely that the early Christians remembered his teaching and faithfully handed down in their words what was substantially true to their mind.

We are not advocating historical scepticism nor brushing aside the historical importance of the gospels. We are realizing better that a gospel is a mixture of fact and interpretation so inextricably interwoven that we have great difficulty in sorting them out. The evangelists bore witness to certain historical facts concerning the man Jesus of Nazareth, born of a woman, who preached, went about doing good, suffered at the hands of his enemies, was crucified and rose from the dead. At the same time the evangelists express the faith of the Christian community in that man whom they believe God has made the Lord and the Christ. They profess their faith, which they show to be rooted in facts of history, namely the events in Jesus' life.

We have now come to the heart of the matter. A gospel is a faith proclamation of the risen Jesus. The risen Jesus is Christ the Lord. He is alive today, living a new life which it is our privilege to share. He is still active and speaking in the Christian community. A gospel is much more concerned with what Jesus is now than with what he was. The evangelists are much more interested in presenting Christ the Lord than in presenting Jesus of Nazareth, though they had not the slightest doubt about his being the same person. In order to present him they did not have to invent anything; they drew upon the eye-witnesses' memory of Jesus in the flesh and interpreted certain events of his life in the light of his present glory without distorting or falsifying facts. Consequently, throughout the gospels we have a double image of Jesus: an image of the risen Jesus super-imposed on the earthly Jesus, the Christ of faith on the historical Jesus. The resurrection experience of the first Christians has coloured the writings of all the gospels. They give us the full truth of Jesus, a thing which no one could possibly have realized during the public ministry. The picture which Caiaphas, the pharisees, Mary Magdalen or even the apostles had of Jesus was not that of the real Jesus. Only after the coming of the Holy Spirit after the resurrection did the apostles learn the full truth of Jesus: 'When the Spirit of truth comes, he will guide you into all the truth' (Jn 16. 13). It was only when they knew the risen glorified Jesus that they understood the meaning and significance of his earthly career.

A contemporary gospel

We are always wanting to learn from the gospels what Jesus really *was*, whereas the evangelists are chiefly occupied in telling us what he really *is*. When we see the implications of the fact that the gospels are a profession of faith of the early Christians and not a biography of Jesus, some Catholics are uneasy. They ask: have the evangelists distorted the real Jesus for purposes of faith? are the miracles factual or symbolic? did Jesus tell those parables we read? are the sayings of Jesus we cherish really his or are they made up by the evangelists? By being forced to ask oneself questions like these are we not already undermining the historical trustworthiness of the gospels and taking away the material for forming a sound judgment about Jesus? The uncertainty introduced by all these inescapable questions alarms some Catholics.

On the other hand, the more thoughtful ones see a tremendous gain in this new understanding of the gospels. We twentieth century Christians are Christians just because we profess that Jesus is the Lord and the Christ, that he is alive today, and that we share his new risen life. We do not worship a great teacher who lived two thousand years ago, but Jesus Christ who is alive now. We feel our unity with those first century Christians who put the stress on the present reality of Christ. Like them we look back to his life in the flesh in order to learn how to live a Christ-like life. Like them we adapt his teaching to our circumstances. Like them we treasure the tradition enshrined in the gospels. We do not ignore the question of historicity as of no importance, but we see that the questions of interpretation and faith are of much greater importance. We come to recognize that the correct question we should continually be asking when reading the gospels is not: did this incident actually take place or did Jesus really say this? but rather: what does this incident or this saying mean to the evangelists in their first century circumstances and what does it mean to us today in our quite different circumstances?

It is difficult for most of us to follow this rule, because we must keep reminding ourselves that we should look for the Christ of today who is speaking to us in these gospel traditions, whereas we have the habit of turning our minds back to a man of two thousand years ago in Palestine. It is difficult for another reason also. We must understand what the ideas expressed in the gospels meant to the evangelists and then find words to express the same ideas in twentieth century England. But what did the kingdom of God, the Son of Man, the Saviour, the Messiah, the Son of God and so on mean to the men of the first century? And what suitable terms would render the same ideas to us today in our quite different culture? Despite the difficulties we have to make the effort to read the gospels in this way; for it is the only way to know the truth about Jesus Christ, and knowing the truth about him is the only way really to know God.

F. SOMERVILLE

What think you of Christ?

Essentially, I see this as an impossible question. There is no answer to a question which reaches beyond the limits of any one man's vision; there is no answer to a question where investigation gives rise only to other questions; there can be no answer to any question which reaches deep into the absolute core of humanity and searches for totality when each man knows it is beyond him.

Yet the question is being constantly asked. Each age has framed it in its own way. From the cry of the primitive church, 'Whom do men say I am' to the pop, 'Jesus Christ, Jesus Christ, Who are you, what have you sacrificed? Jesus Christ Superstar, do you think you're what they say you are?', the question is the same.

The difference between asking 'What think you of Christ', and 'What think you of Pius XII or Henry VIII or Hitler' is that the latter are historical figures whose lives, in a real way closed with their deaths. 'What think you of Harold Wilson, or Edward Heath or Bernadette Devlin' is really an open question because what I think of Heath or Wilson or Devlin will change as they change — they are still in the process of 'becoming'; moreover, my idea of them will change as I change; for I also am 'becoming'.

And so it is with Christ. In one sense Christ is an historical figure bound to a certain geographical location and a certain time span, but in another and much more real way he is present, not only in the history of his time but in the community where he dwells. Christ, unlike us, did not complete his life at death — rather his death marked the realization of a new life, a becoming, a being-made-present in all who want, in some way, however unknowingly, to share it. We become who we are at death — all that Christ is includes all he was in his own history and all he has become and will become for us.

110

Christ is living, Christ is becoming

And so it is not enough for me to ask who is the Christ who walked in Israel, or even who is the Christ of the gospels. If I am a Christian and believe in the resurrection I must also ask who is the Christ of the present, who is Christ in 1972 in Bayswater, in Ulster, in Pakistan, in the Pentecostals. It is not enough that I should ask only intellectual questions, or even theological ones, because I am asking about a living being who lives in a community of persons who find him as much in those who seek for truth in the rejection of social norms and legalism as in those who sit on twelve thrones judging the tribes of Israel. The answer to the question 'Who is Christ' is to be found in life itself — wherever men seek to be true, there Christ can be known. This is the message of the gospels.

Christ is living, Christ is becoming, Christ is community

That is not to discount theology. Theologians must meet Christ today in today's terms and must be able to speak to the living experience of their generation. This is no new challenge as any study of the history of Christology readily shows. It was so right from the beginning. The gospels themselves are much less a reflection on the mortal life of Jesus than a statement about the meaning of Jesus. They are the result of the community's meditation on the meaning of Jesus risen and living in the primitive Church. Later ages found it necessary to ponder the problem of Jesus as consistent with the notion of one, pre-existing God and framed their theology in terms of 'nature' and 'person'. Speculative theology after Chalcedon may have tried to deepen the findings of incarnational theology and formulated the reality of the living Christ in terms of an 'indwelling divinity'. Present day theology, strongly anthropological, harks back to primitive Christology and seeks to ponder anew, in the light of its own experience of the present day world, the meaning and reality of the risen Jesus. In an age which has come to respect dynamism and accept change as a staple of life, Christology has come to look for Christ within human experience and to ask all who would find him to look within the world — 'for there is no where else'.

To place stress on the Jesus of the present is not to deny the Jesus of history — rather it is to affirm that what the gospels declare to be so, really is true. About the literal accuracy of the gospel episodes I'm unconcerned, in so far as my life experience — the living out of my life — does not, at this moment, seem to demand that I know to what, if any, extent the incidents of the gospels — birth, miracles, resurrection — happened literally as they are recorded. More important, but by no means essential, is a conviction that the Christ of the gospels is in some way the same person who was born, lived and died in Israel in those days. But if I were now to be presented with incontrovertible proof that such a figure did not exist and that the Christ of the gospels is a literary composite — a figure of a great reality — I would still like to think that I would believe in the meaning of Jesus. This meaning I see to be an awareness that man can have of the true meaning of his humanity. This awareness is the spirit of Jesus at work in mankind.

But as a Christian — because I was born one and because I have come to affirm positively the truth of Christianity — I believe in the historical Jesus and in the meaning which emerges from a close and informed study of the writings of the New Testament. I believe of the Jesus of the gospels that he was

truly and totally a man

that God spoke to humanity in and through Jesus Christ

so fully that his word was Divine and that Jesus Christ is the Word of God

that the Spirit of Jesus, the Word, lives on in the community. So, to the litany begun earlier — Jesus is living, Christ is becoming, Christ is community — I should like to add that Jesus Christ is man as I know man to be, that Jesus Christ is Word and Son of God.

It follows from this that since God chose to speak his word to man in and through a man, then for the believer to ask the question 'who is Christ' is to ask the question 'who is God?' What we know of God we know through Jesus. In Christ man knows all there is to be known about God and has arrived at the journey's end. 'I am the Way, I am the Truth, I am the Life; no one comes to the Father except by me ... anyone who has seen me has seen the Father'.[1] Padovano's thesis,[2] that God's word, spoken in Jesus Christ was so complete that it is itself divine, and that Jesus Christ is the revelation of the Father in a way nothing else could ever be, I find attractive.

Christ reveals God to us in a way unknown even in the Old Testament. He shows that God is found only in community, 'Where two or three are gathered together', that God comes only to community makers (the second is like to this, 'thou shalt love thy neighbour') and further that he is found in the visible community.

The gospels and the person of Christ show clearly that as the Word of God to man is man, then God is found only in our humanness, that God comes only to those who want to be human, who honestly seek to find themselves. Being human is the most difficult of our undertakings. 'Human experience is so multi-faceted that God spoke his final Word to us through it. Thus the problem of God begins and ends in a Word too human not to have been divine. The problem of God can be summed up in a word we call "Jesus" and God calls "Son".' [3]

And so, inadequately perhaps, because it is of necessity only an outline, the litany ends — Jesus is living, Jesus is becoming, Jesus is community, Jesus is so man that Jesus is God's Son and Word. It would be possible to go on; for in a way all that is, is Jesus, and nothing is without him. I have said nothing here of the implications of all this; yet it is in being able to see and live the implications that we have any chance at all of being Christ-like, 'saved', 'realized', 'humanized', 'divinized'. Until one has explored the implications of the Word of God spoken to the community in Jesus Christ, one has not answered the question in a living way.

Meditation on the meaning of Jesus has been the mission of the Church throughout the ages but the clarity of her vision of the implications of the Word of God spoken to Jesus in the community would seem to have never been clearer than it is now. The Second Vatican Council did not initiate this thinking; it merely recognized and confirmed it. *The constitution on revelation, The constitution on the Church, The decree on*

---

[1] John 14, 6.
[2] Padovano: *Who is Christ.*
[3] Ibid.

ecumenism, The declaration on religious freedom, all spoke in
some way of the implication of the fact that God's word is spoken
in dialogical terms. God's word establishes itself in reciprocity —
as it is in the Trinity, so it is with us. The word is a personal word,
established in communication. Gone are the days of miracles, of
supernatural intervention; for God has entrusted his word to
human beings to share it humanly in their own terms. 'Go teach
all nations' is still the command which Christians hear, but to
speak of Christ is to speak first of and to man in a way man
can hear and understand. The notion of 'readiness for' is as
true of the good news in the more explicit sense as it is for
other forms of learning. To speak of the joy of Christ and the
goodness of God to a trip-addicted, agonizing junkie is as stupid
as to preach the turning of the other cheek and the meekness
of Christ to Bernadette Devlin.

God is no magician, the spirit of Christ no magic. 'Death-
ridden people, the cure of the world lies within the world; only
life is the healer of life'[4] is the cry of prophets like the
Berrigans in our day. Christ is at work in the world 'And that
is where and the only place he can be known'; 'the world cannot
be saved from the outside'; 'all things human are our concern'.[5]

One of the great and comforting things about present day
theology is that it frees us to love — not only a transcendent
God 'out there', but a world which is crying out to be loved and
wept over, a world which contains within itself the seeds of
transformation.

This vision of Christ is too optimistic and borders on the
unreal if it leaves out the meaning of the cross. The cross speaks
not so much of suffering, but of love which is deep enough to
be death. And death was the inevitable for integrity and
humanness such as Christ's. The cross reveals the absoluteness
of God's love and the resurrection communicates this love to us.

As I read back over this I am struck again by the impossibility of trying to answer unanswerables. There is no answer; there
are many answers; there is one answer.

SISTER R. CRUMLIN

---

[4] Daniel Berrigan.
[5] Cf. Paul VI, *Ecclesiam Suam.*

The infancy narratives

Fact or interpretation

Even a brief study of the infancy narratives makes us sadly aware of our superficial understanding of the message they contain. For many they are nothing more or less than the Christmas story. They are often regarded as merely the source of answers to questions about the time, place, visitors and circumstances of the birth of Jesus — questions beginning with 'what', 'where' and 'when'. If this is so, and it would appear to be so in very many cases, judging from the way we repeatedly 'do' the Christmas story as merely a historical account concerned with the details surrounding the birth of the baby Jesus, then the heart of the narratives and the intentions of Matthew and Luke can easily be lost. The meaning of these passages is profound and beautiful. The flesh of interpretation builds a fullness around the bones of historical details.

We must look at these passages, not in the analytical spirit of western mentality but with minds sensitive to the faith and conviction of the writers. These chapters must be treated as theology and the only legitimate questions one ought to ask are theological ones. We should not become anxious about whether we have pure history or not. Whether we like it or not we must be content to live with a measure of uncertainty as to where fact ends and interpretation begins. Fr Hubert Richards writes, 'When a westerner is presented with a story his very first question is almost certain to be, "Did it really happen?" The Semite, when he is told a story asks, "What does it mean?".' The authors of the infancy passages are primarily interested in the significance of their story. Their eye is on the theological meaning of the traditions they are dealing with, and not (as ours is) on their historical accuracy.

The infancy narratives are history written in the light of faith. Many years after the events of the first Holy Week the evangelists understood the birth of Jesus in terms of God's self-

115

revelation in historical happenings. No one, then or now, can see the true significance nor the unsurpassable uniqueness of the man of Nazareth or his birthday without a faith that triumphs over the blindness of flesh. The birth day is only as important as the man whose birth day it is. What is chronologically first must be understood in the light of the later, full revelation. The infancy gospels, composed at a later stage than the gospel which was first preached (beginning in all four gospels with the ministry of John the Baptist and the baptism of Jesus), are an attempt to show the meaning of Christ's life and ministry as foreshadowed in the events of his infancy. They apparently arose in certain areas of the primitive Church and were intended to be theological expansions of the bare data contained in the memory of the early life of Jesus by the use of the Old Testament and of the developed belief in his divine Sonship and his Messiahship. They are proclamations of his supernatural origin and character and anticipations of the revelation of him as Messiah and Lord to both Jews and Gentiles. Their purpose was more profound than simply to relate isolated incidents from Christ's infancy; it was to deepen the faith of the listeners and readers in the meaning of his work. Christ had already been presented in the first preaching of the gospel as the fulfilment of all the Old Testament hopes. But this had dealt only with his public life. The purpose of the infancy gospels is to show that the same was true even of his hidden life.

Matthew and Luke

On a closer look now at the narratives themselves, we find that only Matthew and Luke have given us these accounts. Matthew and Luke have in common only the basic elements of the birth of Jesus in Bethlehem and the virginal conception of Mary. It is hardly possible that they have drawn their material from a common source because there are many differences, which we have since lumped together in addition to some later devotional speculations under the general umbrella of the Christmas story. The fact that Luke does not mention the magi, Herod, or the flight into Egypt, and that Matthew misses out on the annunciation, the nativity and the circumcision should not make us wonder about which of the evangelists is giving us the full

Christmas story but about which aspect of the Christmas event each is endeavouring to express.

The real event that the infancy narratives are based on is the death-resurrection of Christ. Reflecting on this great passover in the spirit of the risen Lord, Matthew was concerned with showing Jesus as the fulfilment of the Old Testament Messianic promises. The word of God's love for men, spoken in various ways and at various times from the first moment of creation right through to the prophets, was spoken definitively in the person of Christ.

Luke's theologizing on the birth of Jesus is also deeply rooted in the resurrection with heavy overtones of the Old Testament. The predominant theme in his mind is the idea of God's supremacy, of God's salvation coming to men, not from men striving for it by their own efforts, not from their own ability and potentialities, but as a gift from God. It would seem that in Luke's plan, the purpose of the infancy narrative is to show that the freely-given Spirit was present in Jesus of the line of David from the first, before showing later in the gospel that his presence was communicated to the apostles, and in Acts, that it was communicated by the apostles to the rest of the world.

With the points just made in mind, let us have a brief look at some of the more well-known events of the infancy narratives.

Gabriel's message

In the annunciation of Gabriel to Mary we have to distinguish between what is definitely affirmed by scripture, that is that God manifested himself to Mary, and the way in which that manifestation took place. The importance of Gabriel lies in his message, not his appearance. The early Church believed that Mary was called by God and knew herself to be called — to play an essential role in God's plan of salvation: to be the mother of his Messiah. This is the essential factor; the manner in which God's will was made known is secondary. Mary's child is to be not only another great prophet, a special Messiah, but THE Messiah. Cardinal Daniélou writes, 'Faith in *a* Messiah is common to both Jews and Christians, but what divides them is the problem of whether the son of Mary is *the* Messiah or not'.

The vital bits of information concerning the annunciation are that the child to be born of Mary would be the expected Messiah, God's only Son and a descendant of David.

Bethlehem

There are variations as to the precise cave, room and so on in which Jesus was born, but the town of Bethlehem itself remains constant in all accounts. It is clear that the fact of Jesus' being born there was considered extremely significant. Luke stresses this by adding that Bethlehem is the 'city of David'. As we have seen, one of the outstanding motifs in the infancy narratives is to show Jesus as the Messiah descended from David. It is no mere accident that Jesus the Messiah, of the House of David, should be born in David's city. Jesus, the second David, was to complete the work of the first. That he was born in a cave is a piece of information not found in the gospels; it is local tradition.

The shepherds

There is no reason to regard the presence of the shepherds on the first Christmas morning as anything but historical. More important, however, is the certain significance attached to their presence by the writer. We have seen how these accounts lay special emphasis on everything that shows Jesus as the Messiah descended from David. Now David was a shepherd from Bethlehem. The story of how David was chosen speaks of his keeping his father's sheep in Bethlehem (I Sam.). To show Jesus being born among the shepherds in Bethlehem was to show him as the new David, another from among the shepherds of Bethlehem, destined to be not just a shepherd of men, but the 'chief shepherd'. And in this context too, perhaps the 'manger' becomes a sign linked with the messianic theme of a shepherd descended from David.

The angelic announcement to the shepherds is to be understood in the same manner as Gabriel's annunciation. The presence of the 'heavenly host' at Jesus' birth is a way of expressing that God was present in the child in the manger; it is a suggestion that the child is divine. For a long time this profound and breathtaking theological statement of Luke, concerning the magnitude of God's love for us, meant nothing more to me than the annual appearance of four winged tinselled creatures who bobbed and swayed on their umbilical threads for two or three weeks of the year. The canticle of the angels, like the other canticles of the narrative, is meant to bring out the spiritual significance of the episode. Luke, doubtless, like his contemporaries, believed in the existence of angels, but, as Fr W. Harrington has recently written, 'his infancy narrative would offer a precarious basis indeed for an argument purporting to *prove* the existence of these heavenly beings. What he has done is to use traditional language and imagery to present and interpret divine realities'.

The magi

It is accepted by scripture scholars today that astrology was called into the services of messianic belief and that there exists a horoscope of the expected king-messiah. In Matthew the 'wise men' declare 'We have seen his star at its rising' and this seems a better translation than 'in the east' — one's horoscope is determined by the start that 'rises' at the moment of one's birth. The 'wise men' could well be Essenes from the Dead Sea shore or from beyond the Jordan who had cast a horoscope of the messiah-king and who were convinced that he had been born. Matthew has taken this tradition, embellished it with miraculous elements such as the moving star, which is something quite incidental to the story since they knew where to go anyway, and developed it in terms of Old Testament passages. For him the magi have become representatives of the Gentiles; he has projected on to Jesus' childhood his rejection by the Jews and the coming of the Gentiles to him. God's mysterious plan was present in Jesus from the beginning. Matthew's purpose is to show Jesus as the true Israel, which is now no longer just the Jewish people, but that to which all nations are called.

Presentation

Because we as adults ask the wrong kind of question concerning the infancy narratives, we consequently tend to supply

children with an incomplete kind of answer. None of us
would regard it as good teaching simply to increase the amount
of detail which we impart, Christmas after Christmas, as the
child grows older. And yet we have tended to do this, even
though in fact this approach will have been neutralized by the
fact that many children will have been introduced to the crib
as soon as to their first rattler or football. It is so easy to miss
the message of the narratives if we begin by explaining that Jesus
is God and then go into details regarding the kind of cave, the
animals there, the clothes of the shepherds, the names, number,
nationality and gifts of the wise men, the miracle of the moving
star, and nothing more. But making the infancy narratives the
occasion of a gradually deeper enrichment of the child's apprecia-
ation of God's love is no easy business. Most of our contemporary
syllabuses offer little help. The Christmas story often seems to
be 'stuck on' to the end of the autumn term's work. How does
one avoid saying the same kind of thing about Jesus with young
children as one has previously said about God in the reception
year? This and similar questions were raised at a recent teachers'
meeting on precisely this problem. We accepted the fact that
our difficulty stemmed from insufficient awareness of the meaning
of the Trinity: that it is *because* of the birth of Jesus, the person
of Jesus, that we can say all we know about God's love, care
and forgiveness. Instead of being a counter-attraction to God,
Jesus is the one who is responsible for our belonging more fully
to him. He is the Way to God, the Window on God, the Face of
God, the Gift of God, the Promise of God. These are the aspects
we try to present from the beginning and hope to deepen as
the years go by. This is the heart of the infancy stories and
instead of 'working them in' at the end of term, we try to
shape the whole autumn term's theme around it for maximum
effect because we are dealing with the central mystery of our
faith, the Incarnation of Christ. "In this is love, not that we
loved God but that he loved us and sent his Son to be the
expiation for our sins".

Infants and juniors

Even when dealing with infants it is necessary to be true to
the gospels, as already outlined, and to begin laying the founda-

tion for a more mature understanding and response later on. This will not be achieved by over-emphasizing the baby with the halo, the friendly little donkey and the cuddly lambs. But it may be achieved by always setting the Christmas event against the background of God the Father. Supposing we take the theme of *thankfulness* — a theme that fits into the mood of autumn and a theme often used with the younger children. We should try first to enkindle and then nourish a sense of gratitude in the essentially self-centred child. As we help him to look at the experiences he lives through we should try to draw out that generosity that gives birth to gratitude and above all we should begin by encouraging gratitude *for* Jesus, the gift to us from his Father, sent to help us. We cannot rest here. The teacher will know how and when to build this into an appreciation of the fact that our thanks to God for all people and things is best expressed *through* Jesus. He is the One who makes the most acceptable kind of thanksgiving to God the Father for us. As soon as possible we should endeavour to weave this expression of thanksgiving through Jesus into the fabric of the Eucharist (Eucharistia meaning thanksgiving). We ourselves are always trying to understand this mystery more fully. We shall never do so completely precisely because it is a mystery, but this is no reason why we should not open to the children right away the opportunity of growing towards a mature understanding of the Trinity, an understanding of the role of Jesus in drawing us towards the Father. This approach is, in fact, more theologically accurate, more educationally defendable and more psychologically suitable than some of our traditional approaches to preparation for First Communion. Our autumn term's theme on thankfulness would culminate in seeing Christmas as the birthday of the Person for whom and then in and through whom our gratitude to God the Father is now and always fully expressed.

Let us have a look at the theme of *belonging* — a theme eminently suitable for the beginning of the school year. We should encourage the children to become aware of the meaning of belonging, the feeling of 'being at home', the sense of 'togetherness' in a family, the security of being the object of the love of the father and mother. As Christmas approaches we should prepare to celebrate the birthday of the Special One, Jesus, who belongs to God and is given to us by God so that he belongs to us also. Again the teacher will know when and how to deepen this knowledge into an appreciation that because of this unique birthday we all belong in a new way to God, we can all feel 'at home' with God because of Jesus, we can all enjoy the privilege and security of calling God 'our Father'. Having discussed this among ourselves and then introduced it into our teaching we were convinced that more children than we imagined in the seven to eight age group were able to appreciate this loving gesture and call from God in the Christmas event and gropingly to change little habits and tendencies in their lives in response to this 'news'.

Once again autumn must be the ideal time for a theme on *gifts*. The land is laden with the harvest of nature's gifts, and the city will soon be filled with the packaged gifts that people will buy for their friends. What better setting for unfolding the Christmas gift of God to men in the person of Jesus, through Mary, and later for deepening this into a realization that a gift is a part of the giver, a sharing of one's self, a sign and an increase of love. Through the gift that is Jesus, through the way he lived his life among people, through the love that showed itself in everything he said and did, we can know the kindness that is in God and then love and serve him in the gift of life that he has given to us.

Think for a moment how you yourselves could draw from the heart of the message in the infancy narratives at Christmastime to reveal the Christian implications in themes such as forgiveness, courage, service and so on for upper juniors. At this age also the occasion of Christmas can be used to appreciate the significance of Jesus in investigations into themes such as the Bible, signs and symbols, change, growth, the Church. It is felt that this use of themes and this approach towards Christmas will guarantee a true imparting of the details of the infancy narratives and will provide a sound and sure preparation for the reception of the three sacraments entered into during these junior years — the three great meetings with the love of this God-man who was born on the first Christmas morning.

Secondary pupils

A detailed outline covering a special approach to be presented at a certain age must surely have an artificial ring about it. Rather than discuss variations of the incidents in the infancy narratives (which of course include the genealogy of Jesus, the presentation and finding in the Temple) and their suitability for definite age-groups, I prefer to develop an approach to the explanation of the incident which will depend on the theme followed and the questions asked. The theme of *fulfilment* is suggested — Matthew's motif in the infancy narratives concerning the completion of the line of promise, Jesus and the new Adam, the second David and so on — as suitable in the secondary school because of the more developed sense of time and history at this age.

As against this, I was privileged to take part in a junior school pageant through the media of song, dance, mime drama and reading on precisely this theme. It involved some of the lower juniors; it moved swiftly; it followed the lines of the gradual self-revelation of God from creation to his final Word fully spoken in Jesus; it ended (after 'Lord of the Dance', of course), with children, parents and teachers sharing the Eucharist. It would be rash to say that it had no real meaning for the children. However, I feel that it will have an increased significance in the secondary school and many secondary syllabuses try to build their treatment of the Christmas event around this rich motif. It is at this age that we can enter into a more serious treatment of the infancy narratives because this is the time when many begin to reject a very literal interpretation of the facts in the infancy gospels and sometimes of 'facts' that have no scriptural foundation. It is very encouraging to see the understanding with which the true meaning of the magi's visit, for instance, is received by the teenager, to feel the dawning of a new insight into that time-worn visit, never seriously considered since childhood, particularly with its implications for these days of ecumenism and the study of comparative religion.

Space does not permit a fuller expression of what is felt concerning the treatment of this topic at secondary level. These days there is much help provided for the teacher who wishes to communicate the message of Christmas through the media of art, drama, music, mime and so on. With fifth and sixth formers the emphasis will be on discussion but it presumes that we ourselves are fairly confident in and grateful for the 'goodness' contained in the infancy 'news'.

Finally

We have many things to teach our children, but really only one great truth of the love of God for man expressed in the saving mystery of Christ our Lord. Everything draws its meaning and fullness from this centre. Whether we are involved with the sacraments or the commandments, the liturgy or sin, we can never lose sight of the fact that they are explained in the light of Jesus Christ. Rightly or wrongly I feel that when we come to 'explain' the birthday of the man Jesus, the Christ of the gospel, to our children, we shall be on the right lines if we remember all the time this image of the Son, the Face of the Father, the Window on God, the Personification of divine Love.

In *The constitution on revelation* we find reference to Jesus the revelation of the Father and the fulfilment of God's promise 'through his whole work of making himself present and manifesting himself, through his words and deeds, his signs and wonders, but especially through his death and glorious resurrection from the dead and final sending of the Spirit of truth'. It is in the light of this knowledge and faith that Matthew and Luke wrote their infancy narratives and it is in the light of the same knowledge and faith that we must understand them and unfold them to our children. The presence of this same 'Spirit of truth' will give us confidence in our efforts.

DONAL J. O'LEARY

The life and ministry of Jesus

The gospels were written by Christians for Christians, by men of faith for men of faith. You learn to understand their language only by studying the cultural and religious situation of that generation of Christians who produced our written gospels. If we change from taking the view of the gospels as exact reports of what actually happened to seeing them as proclamations of faith in the risen Christ present among us, then we have to re-think nearly everything in the gospels. In this essay I wish to do no more than indicate some of the areas where re-thinking is called for.

The infancy narratives

We need to recall how the infancy stories were eventually put together. The Acts of the Apostles makes quite clear that the earliest preaching of the gospel began with the baptism of Jesus. The stories of his earlier life are a later addition. 'It is a recognized phenomenon of popular literature — and it is in this class that the gospels fall — that stories about the childhood of a hero begin to be told later than the stories about his time of greatness; obviously people must have their attention attracted by his achievements before they begin to ask about his boyhood. This does not, of course, say that the stories of his boyhood are false, but only shows that they are likely to have been composed from a different angle, and with more developed and mature thought about the hero'. (H. Wansborough, O.S.B., *The Clergy Review*, February 1970, p. 112).

The evangelists, when writing their gospels, know the end of their story: the risen Lord in glory. When writing about the beginning of Jesus' life, they want to tell us that their gospel is not about ordinary human affairs but about someone who is God-with-us.

St Matthew's stories of the infancy contain definite elements
to be found in folk-literature, for example wicked kings, oriental
magicians, appearances of a star. This suggests that the author
does not intend his readers to believe he is relating actual historical events. Matthew invented the story of the magi which
is primarily theological in interest and purpose; Jesus is
recognized by the Gentiles but not by his own people, the Jews.
Matthew created the star of Bethlehem. Most evident of all is
his effort to present Jesus as the new Moses (see above cited
article by Fr Wansborough).

Luke reflected upon different Old Testament texts to present
Jesus to his readers. He is not concerned to tell us how Jesus
was born but rather who he was, with stress on the divinity.
His story of the birth of Jesus is based on the infancy story of
Samuel (1 Sam. 1-2). The census associated by Luke with
Quirinius, governor of Syria, is not a historical fact. When he
says that at Bethlehem 'there was no room at the inn' he is
probably thinking of the future poverty and renunciation of
Jesus rather than of any inhospitality or full house. It is quite
possible that there were shepherds in the region where Jesus
was born, but 'there is no doubt a contrast intended between
shepherds, the poor and ignorant, and the leaders of Judaism'
(J. McKenzie, *Dictionary of the Bible,* s.v. shepherds).

Christ's boyhood and youth

We know nothing of the first thirty years of Jesus' life. It
is true that Luke tells a story of his going to the Temple at
Jerusalem; but it may well be that the evangelist is describing
the youth of Jesus in terms of the young Samuel who grew in
wisdom and in stature and in favour with the Lord and with
men.

Born a Jew he went through the ordinary process of growing
up like any other Jewish boy. His thoughts were Jewish. His
years at Nazareth were his formative years during which he read
and reflected on the Old Testament, and this, together with his
pious parents' care, explains how he grew in the knowledge of
God. To speak of his divinity apart from this completely human
context and to think he did not have to learn about God is
implicitly to deny his humanness.

Paul and the author of the letter to the Hebrews say that Jesus was sinless. Jesus himself, according to John, challenges his opponents: 'Can one of you convict me of sin?' The evangelists found him so very good a man intent on doing God's will that they took for granted he was sinless. So do Christians. Because it was a human goodness, it was not without a struggle and strain.

The baptism of Jesus

Jesus insisted upon being baptised by John. We do not know what actually happened, about the voice of the Father or the appearance of a dove; for as usual the story is turned into a theological reflection on Jesus the Christ.

We do not know how Jesus himself understood his own baptism. We have only the interpretation of the evangelists. The baptism of Jesus is a watershed of the old and the new age. To the first Christians, steeped in the Old Testament, the baptism of Jesus announced the beginning of a new Israel, of a new mankind and of a new messianic age. It is interpreted as Christ's public acceptance of his calling to be the Messiah who would save mankind by suffering and death, as had been foretold in Isaiah of the Servant of Jahweh. It was not the vocation itself; for he had been called from birth to be Saviour; but in some religious experience at the Jordan he becomes more clear in his own mind what his role in life is to be and he publicly manifests his acceptance for the first time. The voice from heaven signifies the Father's election of Jesus as his chosen one. The mention of the Spirit, symbolised by a dove, reminds us of the spirit of God poetically pictured in Genesis as brooding over the waters at the origin of the world and of man; Jesus coming out of the Jordan waters is about to begin his task of bringing life and order to the world.

Writing after the resurrection the evangelists see the baptism of Jesus as having some connection with his passover. It is a symbolic pre-representation of what would happen to him. Jesus is reported (Mk 10. 38) as saying that he has a baptism with which is to be baptized, a term used metaphorically of his passion and the beginning of a new life or state. The baptism and the temptation in the desert are to be understood as one event; this is how the gospel writers intended them to be taken. The early Christians saw the intrinsic unity of the baptism and temptation and used it to instruct in the significance of Christian baptism.

Having accepted his messianic calling the man Jesus examines himself on how he has to do his work. He sees the old world is ending and he has to play his part in ushering in the new world, the spiritual kingdom of God on earth. He sees that he has to carry out his vocation through suffering and firm adherence to God's will. Matthew teaches this truth by portraying Jesus as facing up to temptations to follow any other course; and Matthew chooses three temptations which the old Israel had failed to overcome, which are also types of dangers which ever confront the members of the Church.

The temptation story is placed at the beginning of the public ministry, but we must not think, as many good Christians do, that Jesus was left free of the devil until Gethsemane. He was truly human and shared our weakness; he was 'in every respect tempted as we are' (Heb. 4. 15), though he did not succumb to the enticements of sin. He must have frequently during his ministry experienced temptations to turn aside from the way of life determined for him by the Father. Moreover, the very great insistence by the New Testament writers on the obedience of Jesus to the Father's will suggests that he was like us in the matter of temptation; for obedience would be very easy to anyone never tempted to disobey.

Preaching the kingdom

The God-problem — how to think and speak intelligibly of God — is present to every generation. Jesus had to handle it. He reflected deeply on the one he could call 'Abba' and came to fasten upon one aspect which he made central to his teaching. This was the idea of God's kingly rule. It was not original; for it had an Old Testament background: Yahweh is overlord of Israel, full of care and concern for his people.

The kingdom is not a place; it is a personal relationship. God gives himself to men in friendship and asks for a return. It is a gift inasmuch as God generously takes the initiative; and it is a demand or challenge in so far as God, entering into a man's life, calls him to change his previous way of life.

Jesus, through his experience of life, grew in consciousness that God's kingly rule was present in himself. The baptism-temptation experience was one high moment in that growing consciousness. His calling men to be his disciples suggests that he was aware of himself as living the life of the kingdom. When he saw the mounting opposition to him, he felt that the fate of ancient prophets was likely to befall him, but he resolved that nothing, not even death, was going to stop him from preaching the kingdom. He probably shared the confusion of his contemporaries about the time when the kingdom would be completed, but he was absolutely sure he could already call God 'Abba', he believed in a resurrection (cf. the answer to the Sadducees, Mt. 22. 23-32) and a future life (cf. his imagery of a heavenly banquet, Mt. 8. 11 and *passim*).

In his preaching Jesus made known that God's kingly rule is already present and still to come; in other words it is in process of coming. It is already present in the midst of men, because it is inseparable from his own person; indeed it is most clearly visible in his person and works. He teaches that it is now lowly and hidden but transforming. Jesus, however, more frequently speaks of its future aspect when it will be complete and fully visible. The *Our Father* is a prayer of expectation.

Jesus invited men to enter the kingdom. They were to do so by becoming his disciples; but for this they must first bring about in themselves a radical change of heart. Then he makes high demands upon them, demands of love which may be heroic at times. He does not lay down any law at all, because law cannot cater for the demands of love. What he does say all the time is that if you are the child of God you must want to do the will of your Father, and you will do this if you try to be like me. And from the gospels we see that Jesus' consuming love for the Father showed itself in his doing the Father's will and in his selflessly serving his fellowmen.

The parables

The parables of Jesus are his preaching, not simply illustrations of some doctrine. A parable is a story or action which conveys a truth in a concrete, vivid and pictorial manner. Jesus, like all other teachers in the East, spoke to his audience in concrete rather than abstract terms. In spite of the difficult text of Mark 4. 10-12 it is ridiculous to suggest that Jesus used parables to hide his doctrine and mystify his hearers. If he had wanted to do this, it would have been simpler to say nothing at all.

The evangelists felt free to adapt the parables as they pleased in order to provide lessons for the different kinds of Christians in the primitive Church. We can see this adaptation as we read them; for example, the parable of the lost sheep in Matthew 18, 12-14 is a story about joy, but in Luke 15. 3-7 the same parable is given a quite different context, namely Jesus' answer to a complaint that he associated with bad characters. The evangelists showed both fidelity and flexibility in adapting the parables: fidelity to the major themes of Jesus' teaching and flexibility in altering them for the current life of the Church and of the individual Christian. A straightforward reporting of the original parable as Jesus uttered it would have been useless in the changed situation.

As we read them today we ourselves should remember to adapt them to our twentieth century situation in this country.

The miracles of Jesus

We must dismiss from our minds the popular notion of miracle as some startling happening contrary to the laws of nature. Jesus was opposed to them in this sense (Matt. 7. 22; Mk 8. 11; Lk. 23. 8; Jn 4. 48).

A miracle is some extraordinary event which is recognized by faith as a work of God. It is not faith that makes it a work of God; but faith must be present in a person for him to see that it is a work of God. This presence of faith and act of God distinguish miracles from the extraordinary works done by many genuine wonder-workers throughout history.

One thing distinguishes Jesus' miracles. He insists upon faith in himself. He cannot work miracles except in the context of faith; thus Mark says explicitly he could do no mighty work at Nazareth because of the people's unbelief. As he works in the name of God his Father and on God's authority, the faith he demands is directed to himself in whom the power of God is active.

Jesus' miracles are not proofs of his divinity, as the old apologists used to claim. They are signs; signs that the kingdom of God was in process of coming (Lk 11. 20) and showing what the kingdom is like. Those who come to Jesus in faith come to the one in whom the kingdom is already established.

After the resurrection the disciples told about the extraordinary things which Jesus did. The stories were coloured in the telling before the evangelists wrote them down. The miracles were preached, and the hearers were invited to have a part in them; for the stories contained lessons for Christian living.

The same is true today. The miracle stories in the gospels are addressed to us. They challenge our faith in Christ and are meant for our instruction. So our first question should not be: what actually happened? did he really turn water into wine? did he really walk on the water? Our first and main question should be: what does it mean to me? What is the point of the miracle story of the water at Cana?

Jesus continues to work his miracles today. He works them in us and through us, his disciples. He had once said: 'You will do greater things than I do'. If we hold by the true meaning of miracle — an extraordinary event recognized by faith as an act of God — we shall understand that whenever we increase faith and hope and love in the world, when we bring back a sinner to God, we are working a miracle, giving a sign that the kingdom of God is among us and showing what it is like.

The passion and death

The amount of space devoted by the evangelists to the narratives of the passion and death of Jesus shows that they considered this story the most important of all the gospel stories.

These narratives are not so much factual accounts of what happened as theological reconstructions in the light of the Old Testament. The post-resurrection evangelists knew that the humiliation and death of the Messiah would be a great scandal

to the Jews, and so the writers wanted to show that the tragedy
had been announced in the scriptures. Study, for example, the
frequent use made of Ps. 21 in the stories. Four strange pheno-
mena of nature are reported as taking place at the crucifixion,
three of which are explained as fulfilment of scripture.

When reading the narratives of the passion and death it is
misleading to have in mind analogies of justice, ransom, repara-
tion, satisfaction, buying back. These judicial and legalist notions
may have been useful in ancient days, but in order to understand the reality of what happened we have to think in terms
of *love*. On the cross Jesus manifests God's love for men and
men's sinfulness. Men have become estranged from God by their
sins. No legal procedure can effect true reconciliation. The guilty
must be forgiven. And forgiveness can be had only from God
by a free gift of grace. God's love which is in Jesus Christ was
declared in the cross. Men were reconciled with God and
brought into a new relationship with him. See 1 Jn 4. 9; Jn 3.
16-17; 1 Jn 4. 16-19; 1 Jn 3. 16; 1 Jn 15. 3; 14. 31.

It would be helpful and accurate to think of Jesus as the
representative of God and the representative of man. In his
ministry Jesus was the human expression of God's love, and he
forgave sinners and sought them out. The cross was the climax
of his ministry, showing God's love to the uttermost in willing
to lay down his life for his enemies. Jesus was also our representative. Sin has a social character; we are all involved in it,
so that no man is solely responsible for his own sins nor entirely
innocent of the sins of others. Jesus identified himself with men
in their need and lostness. 'Christ died for our sins', not as
our substitute but as our representative. By his suffering and
death he embodies our putting love in place of rebellion. In the
cross all Christians see the central mystery of our redemption.

The resurrection

How are we to think and speak of the resurrection? The
accounts in the gospels are inconsistent and logically conflicting;
for instance did Christ appear first in Galilee or in Jerusalem?
Scholars have for generations tried to harmonize or reconcile the
accounts and have always failed. It is surely significant that
the evangelists were not in the least worried about the inconsisten-

cies and felt no desire to modify their accounts for the sake of uniformity or harmony.

The resurrection stories are professions of faith in the risen Jesus; they are vehicles for conveying the evangelists' belief that Jesus is now alive after dying. They give 'gospel truth', that is, truth known by faith rather than by reason.

The empty tomb is a vividly pictorial way of expressing faith that Christ is risen. Faith in the resurrection does not depend on some one having seen the tomb empty. If the evangelists were deeply convinced that Jesus is now alive, they could easily argue that he must have risen from the dead and therefore the tomb must be empty.

There are discrepancies in the appearances, due no doubt to the theological purpose of the evangelists. A common feature seems to be that the apparition (Jesus) is not immediately recognizable. It took some time to establish identity. It is not Jesus who has changed; it must, then, be the witnesses who have changed.

People usually conclude from the empty tomb that Jesus rose bodily, that is, with the same body he had before. But such a conclusion is not conclusive. From the scriptural texts you cannot *prove* the bodily resurrection of Jesus. Moreover, if we tried to find out what the New Testament writers think of bodily resurrection, we should find they had a variety of ideas (cf. *Dictionary of Biblical Theology*, s.vv. body, resurrection). Paul, for example, might have been embarrassed if he had read some of the gospel accounts, such as that of the risen Jesus eating; he was at pains to contrast a physical and a spiritual body (1 Cor. 15), this latter denoting a completely different mode of existing with identity of personality before and after death.

F. SOMERVILLE

Learning
from the parables

The parables of Jesus, representing as they do so important a part of the gospel teaching, are singularly difficult to study in a twentieth century classroom. What do we do with them generally? First, we study the Palestinian background of the parable which must be known to us if we are to grasp its meaning; secondly, we read the parable against its background; and thirdly, we explain what it means.

It sounds very simple, but in practice difficulties abound. The parables grow out of a way of thinking which is alien to our western European mentality. It is a way of thinking in pictures, a way of not only conveying but even conceiving truth in a concrete, vivid and pictorial manner. There is nothing elementary or childish about this. It is the way of wisdom and of intuition rather than of ratiocination; it demands a certain stillness of mind and a deep contact with the basic realities, the fundamental experiences of human living — and our twentieth century encourages neither. Computers do not think in parables, and computers are held up for our admiration as ideal thinking machines. So when we read a parable in the classroom it follows that we ourselves are asked, and we ask our adolescents, to enter into a mode of thinking which is not habitually either ours or theirs. This is our first difficulty.

The second difficulty is that we have to ask them also to enter into a framework of living which is not their own. The Palestinian way of life was agricultural and simple, dominated by the routine tasks of field and vineyard, fishing-ground and household, saved from monotony by the simple festivals of wedding and funeral, of harvest rejoicings and of religious worship. This is all very remote and unreal to our fourteen-year-olds in this country, and they are not necessarily prepared to make the effort required to transpose themselves into so alien a setting. Frankly, they are not interested in the way a vineyard was culti-

vated in the time of Christ, or the conventions of a marriage
feast, or the way of a shepherd with his sheep. Ten-year-olds
may be interested in this; because everything about the way
other people live is interesting when you are ten. But our
adolescents will be bored — either obviously and vocally and
obstreperously bored, or passively and docilely bored according
to the behaviour patterns which predominate in their particular
environment. This is our second difficulty.

And then, when we have struggled against these odds to
build up the background and read the parable against this
background, we proceed to explain what it means. In this very
effort we disclose our occidental mentality. An oriental would
not need to explain what it means: the image speaks. The only
parallel I can find to this in our twentieth century experience is
the response of young people to song. The song speaks directly
and at depth; no one is foolish enough to think that he must
try to say otherwise than in song what the song means. To make
the attempt would be to diminish the song. But we persist,
where the parables are concerned, in assuming that we haven't
thought the thing through until we have formulated it in abstract
terms. So we explain what the parable means. And to our
adolescents it is as though an elephant has laboured to bring
forth a mouse. After all, they feel, if you wanted to say that the
effect of God's word upon us will depend upon the disposition
of heart with which we listen to it, why not say so straight out
instead of spending all this time on men sowing seeds in a
remote and unfamiliar situation. This is what we get for trying
to explain the situation to them; and the total experience has
been far from exhilarating.

What can we do in the face of these difficulties? In the first
place, we need to establish clearly and firmly, both in our own
minds and for our pupils, that with the parables we move right
out of the realm of logic into the realm of poetry. Why, after all,
did Jesus teach in parables? We say that he taught in parables
to make it easier for his hearers to understand; but they did not
understand; over and over again we are explicitly told that they
failed to understand what he meant. Some say that Jesus taught
in parables to prevent his hearers from understanding; in that
case it would seem easier for him to have kept quiet. We say
that Jesus taught in parables because it was the traditional

oriental way of teaching. Do we realize that this means, not just
that Jesus would choose to express himself in this way because
it was a way familiar to his hearers, but that he himself would
instinctively think in this way ... he was an oriental. Why did
Jesus speak in parables? Could it be that he could find no
other way of expressing the ineffable? After all, the parables are
extended metaphors. Why do we use metaphor? Sometimes,
admittedly, for mere embellishment of style. But the true use of
metaphor is that to which we are driven by the struggle for self-
expression. Words fail us, we struggle for images, for analogies;
we say: 'It is as though....' 'It is as though ...'— but this
is precisely the introductory formula of the parables. Dr Joachim
Jeremias has pointed out that our translation 'The kingdom of
heaven is like unto ...' is not strictly true to the original. 'The
Aramaic formula', he says, 'is an abbreviation, and should not
be translated "It is like", but "It is the case with the kingdom of
heaven as with...." ' (In other words, 'It is as though....').
In Matt. 13, he points out, the kingdom of heaven is not in fact
like a merchant, but like a pearl; not 'like to maidens', but like
a wedding; not 'like a household', but like a distribution of
wages; not 'like a man who sowed good seed', but like a harvest.
'In all these cases', he says, 'we shall avoid error by remembering that behind the "is like" there lies an Aramaic expression
which we must translate, "It is the case with the kingdom of
heaven as with...." ' Or more simply, 'It is as though....'?
'It may well be', concludes Dr Jeremias, 'that this point is of
great importance for the interpretation of the parables'.
(J. Jeremias: *Rediscovering the Parables,* S.C.M. Press, pp. 79-
80). I find it of considerable importance in the classroom
situation.

For once we have established that the parables are metaphors
we can appeal to parallels in literature and song to show what
happens when a man is driven to metaphor to express what
otherwise is inexpressible. In the first place, no abstract formula
can say all that the metaphor suggests; it has the power to
communicate experience which is beyond computer logic. What
answer can the computer give to the question: 'What is the
colour of loving?' I imagine that any computer into which you
fed that question would jam! The song can answer it: 'All
colours and more'— but in the language of song, not in an

abstract formula. The parable is much nearer to song. This is particularly important in the case of those parables which speak to us of the nature of the Father. How can Jesus possibly find a formula to express the infinity of the Father's mercy as he perceives it? He cannot; so he seeks for images; he says: 'It is as though a man had two sons. . . . It is as though a shepherd had a hundred sheep. . . .'

Secondly, in the struggle to find expression through metaphor there will often be a kind of untidiness, a heaping of image upon image, an unreasonableness, a defiance of the laws of logical argument; poetry, like parable, moves in a world of its own. Take Mark Antony in Shakespeare's *Antony and Cleopatra*, for example: how can the dramatist convey the keen rankling humiliation of this experienced warrior as he sees himself so diminished by his passion for Cleopatra that those who hung upon his very gesture are now deserting him for that novice in the art of war, the young Octavius Caesar,

'The hearts' — he says —
'That spaniel'd me at heels, to whom I gave
Their wishes, do discandy, melt their sweets
On blossoming Caesar; and this pine is bark'd,
That over-topp'd them all.'

What an illogical piling of image upon image! First, in the one word "spaniel'd" is the image of the fawning house-dog, fed on sweetmeats from the table of his Elizabethan master. And then the vigorous 'do discandy' — and the very sweetmeats for which he cringed are spewed up in rejection of the one who fed them to him; he transfers his allegiance, and 'melts his sweets' upon another. And this other is 'blossoming Caesar', with all the suggestion the epithet brings of spring-time freshness and the hope of fruit to come. And the last great, sad image, with its falling cadence, of the loftiest tree in the pine-forest blazed for felling: 'and this pine is bark'd that over-topp'd them all. . . .'

This is sophisticated poetry, of course, and the parables are not sophisticated, but simple; yet we find the same piling of image upon image, as many parables strive to express the same truth. To stress that the parables are metaphors may seem a complication, but in fact it results in a great simplification. For

J

we see that the great number of parables in Jesus' teaching does not necessarily mean a great variety of ideas. On the contrary, it becomes clear that Jesus was never tired of expressing the central ideas of his message in constantly changing images, and those central ideas stand out the more clearly once we realize this. Moreover, if we emphasize that the parables are metaphors, apparent illogicalities are seen to have a logic of their own. Of course it was illogical of the master of the vineyard to pay the same wages to the latecomers as to the first labourers in the vineyards; of course it was illogical of the father to feast his wastrel son and welcome him home as though he had brought honour rather than discredit to his family; of course it was illogical of the shepherd to leave his flock of ninety-nine, for whom he was responsible, and go chasing after the weak and foolish one which had got itself into trouble. These images are struggling to express something which goes way beyond logic, and that is the goodness and generosity of our heavenly Father which are not measured by our standards of the decorous. And finally, to emphasize that the parables are metaphors protects us from the tendency to allegorize. You don't do this with metaphors. When Mark Antony says 'this pine is bark'd that over-topp'd them all' you do not begin to ask what the pine-cones stand for!

In any case, I have found a quickening of interest among teenagers when I suggested that Christ spoke in parables because he was trying to say something terrific — so terrific that he couldn't find words to say it in, and had to look for images. Had he lived today he might well have used song. The fact that Christ tried so hard to say it, that he had so many bashes at it, so to speak, seems to make it worth our while trying hard to grasp it.

But what can we do about the unfamiliar background? Some teachers get over this difficulty by paraphrasing the parable, dressing it up in modern dress, transferring it to an equivalent modern situation, so that the parable of the good samaritan becomes the story of the Mod who was beaten up by thugs and cared for by a Rocker. I know teachers who do this very well, but I am not sure that it is a good idea for the *teacher* to do this. That the pupil should do it at a later stage in the lesson to express under a modern image whatever insight he has into the meaning of the parable is a different thing. The value of a book like *God is for Real, Man* lies in the fact that it was not written by a teacher but by his 'pupils'. No one would claim that the modernized versions so produced express a complete grasp of the parable; they present partial but authentic insights. But if the *teacher* does this he risks passing on to his pupils only *his* partial insight; *he* decides what the parable means, and then finds a story of his own to express it. This is hardly playing fair. The ideal would seem to be that whoever taught these youngsters when they were nine or ten should have gone very thoroughly into the biblical background, so that all that is needed is a reminder to bring it to their consciousness. If this hasn't been done, one possibility is to get two or three of the fairly able boys and girls in the class to work it out (it is quite straightforward and there are plenty of good sources available) and present it to the class. They will listen to one another where they would not listen to the teacher. And then the adult will be able to open up for them and with them that other kind of background which is not less important to the understanding of the parable — the background of human experience. To enter into the parable of the lost sheep, for example, we need not only to know something about the relationship between sheep and shepherd in Palestine, but also to reflect a little on what it means to us, today, to have lost something. This is far more important, and far more often it is ignored.

And what does the parable mean? Here we come to our third difficulty, the fact that our pupils feel, when we have formulated the meaning of the parable, that it wasn't worth all that trouble. We shall have already discovered that it is not really possible to formulate fully the meaning of the parable any more than you can express the meaning of a song without the song itself. Have we therefore to leave it vague, to leave the interpretation to each one as a purely subjective thing? No; the parables do not interpret themselves. Some clue must be sought if their precise point as metaphors is to be seized, and the individual here needs the help of the community. The clue will be found as a rule in the gospels themselves, from which we are often able to discover both what the parables meant to the people to whom Jesus spoke them, and what they meant to the early Church. From this we are able to see that the parables are so rich that they can in fact apply differently to different situations of life. The

context will sometimes reveal this to us. Take, for example,
the parable of the lost sheep. In St Luke it has this introduction:
'The tax-collectors and sinners, meanwhile, were all seeking his
company to hear what he had to say. And the Pharisees and the
scribes complained: "This man", they said, "welcomes sinners
and eats with them." So he spoke this parable to them. . . .' And
the parable concludes with the maxim: 'So there shall be joy
before the angels of God upon one sinner doing penance. . . .'
So we see that the parable, as related by Jesus, was very closely
connected with the drama of Jesus' own life and his proclamation of the kingdom. The Pharisees and scribes were scandalized
by Jesus' accessibility to 'tax-collectors and sinners', and Jesus
had to show them that the kingdom of heaven is like that because
God is like that — essentially and infinitely merciful, the refuge
of the helpless and the weak. But in St Matthew the parable is
given quite a different context. It occurs in chapter 15 as part
of a special instruction given to the *disciples*, guiding them
in their task of governing the kingdom of God. Its conclusion
is quite different: 'It is never the will of your Father in heaven
that one of these little ones should be lost'. Here we see what
happens when the revelation contained in the parable — a
revelation of the infinite love and mercy of the heavenly Father
towards the weak and unprotected, — meets the situation of
the early Church; for that is what St Matthew is concerned with.
Both the context and the conclusion make of it an exhortation
to pastoral care. Since God is thus, so must those whom he
has placed as shepherds over his Church care for the weakest
of their flock. The parable has not been twisted; its central
revelation is the same. But catechesis is the encounter between
the word of God and a human situation. When the situation is
different, the same word will have a different resonance. What
does this same central revelation of the mercy of God say to
our contemporary scene? That will be for our youngsters themselves to discover.

I have been suggesting, I hope, through all this a kind of
classroom method. First, I should be inclined to treat not one
parable in isolation, but a group of parables concerned with the
same central revelation; but only one of them would I explore in
detail. If, for example, I were associating the parables of the
lost coin, the lost sheep and the lost son, I might decide to

explore in detail the second. Then we would establish the fact that Jesus is here seeking for metaphors to express something important that he cannot say otherwise; and this might be illustrated from poetry or song according to the level of the group. Then, since all these parables are about losing things or people, we might explore the sense of loss — what a nuisance it is to lose even something relatively unimportant, the empty feeling it gives us, how we tend to search restlessly until we find it. Then two or three members of the class, who have been primed beforehand, present the Palestinian background. Then we read the parable . . . in St Luke and St Matthew. They hunt for the differences between the two accounts: I offer some explanation of the differences. We discover that the central idea in the parable is the same, but that it meant different things to the Pharisees and the early Church, because their circumstances were different. Our circumstances are different still: what does it mean to us? And the class would break up into groups to discuss this question.

My concern throughout this article has been with what we can help our pupils to learn from the parables. A final word may be appropriate on what we ourselves have to learn as teachers. We have to learn not so much a teaching method as an approach. It is of course commonly said: 'Yes, Jesus gave us an example here; he made his teaching interesting by using stories; we must use stories too'. But there is far more to it than this. For one thing, when you examine the parables you find that they are by no means all good stories. 'The kingdom of heaven is like the yeast a woman took and mixed with three measures of flour till it was leavened all through. . . .' Where is the story there? No; pedagogically Jesus' parables are remarkable not so much for their narrative skill as for their closeness to life. Here is a catechesis from life indeed! And yet even when we have said that we may get it wrong. We say: Jesus chose images from the everyday life of his people to bring the truths of God home to them. But that suggests a Jesus standing apart from life, and choosing deliberately to use life-experience as a kind of divine condescension to the needs of man — to our earthiness and our stupidity. And that isn't how it was. Jesus was involved in life, more fully involved than any of us will ever be. He loved life, and he loved people, and he loved his heavenly Father; and that is why at every turn he saw the drama of salvation mirrored in human living; he was sensitive to the analogies with the divine of which our human experience is full, because man is truly made to the image and likeness of God, and all things speak of the kingdom to those who have eyes to see. If only we had something of the love-warmed vision of Jesus we too should see parables everywhere — but literally everywhere. Biblical scholars suggest that Jesus took some of his parables from the news bulletin, or its Palestinian equivalent, that the parables of the good samaritan, of the burglar, of the man who found bad seed sown by his enemy in his field, were based on actual happenings, on things that were in the news. Why should we not do likewise? But to teach in this way we need the sensitivity to the human situation which Jesus had, and which is revealed in so many pages of the gospel; and we need the sensitivity to the action of God which comes to us in prayer. We need, that is to say, both deep faith and great love. . . .

SISTER RUTH DUCKWORTH

The miracles of Jesus

Miracles as ridiculous

The miracles of Christ, the 'signs' of Christ, as they are called in the New Testament, present a number of difficulties we may tend to overlook. Take one example. According to the ordinary definition of miracles, the person who ought to be most impressed by them and subsequently drawn to Christ, is the agnostic. In fact, the opposite happens; he simply rejects the miracles as ridiculous.

Some Christians are also rather embarrassed by the miracles; with the present emphasis on the humanity of Christ, on the fact that he was truly one of us, they would prefer a Christ who did not work miracles; a miracle-working Christ somehow no longer seems truly human.

Then, miracles cause difficulties to children. Young children already have a 'magic mentality', from which education is supposed to wean them. Will not an emphasis upon miracles simply aggravate that mentality? As for senior pupils, rendered *blasé* by the miracles of modern scientists, they are quite unimpressed by the miracles of Christ. What is walking on the water compared to walking in space? The New Testament miracles seem poor stuff compared to the marvels that men are able to do today.

These factors among others show the need we have to think once more about the miracles of Jesus, especially their nature and their purpose.

Miracles as something uncanny

Let us approach the matter as it might present itself to somebody reading the gospel for the first time. No one reading through the first ten chapters of St Mark could fail to notice that almost half the sentences have some reference to the miracles, either direct or indirect. Constantly you come across phrases like: 'They were astonished', 'They were amazed', 'What is this?,' 'We have never seen the like', 'This man must be possessed', 'Who can this be?', 'They were afraid', 'They all followed him', 'Everyone's searching for you' and so on. This mixture of wonder and awe, of attraction and fear at the same time, conveys accurately the feelings that anyone would have when in contact with something uncanny. Clearly, Mark is presenting us with something out of the ordinary.

The question that immediately poses itself is whether this is what miracles are really about. Are they meant to be a kind of celestial fireworks designed to make people gape in astonishment and awe and overwhelm them with wonder? Yet that is utterly inconsistent with the other sentences accompanying the references to miracles. In chapter one, there is a demoniac: 'I know who you are', he says to Christ, 'you are the holy one of God'. 'Be quiet', says Christ, 'Come out of him', forbidding him to proclaim who he is (1. 25). In the same chapter there are several demoniacs: 'He would not allow them to speak because they knew who he was' (1. 34). Later on in the chapter he speaks to some lepers whom he heals: 'Mind you say nothing to anyone', he tells them as they go off (1. 44). In chapter three it is said of the unclean spirits: 'He warned them strongly not to make him known' (3. 12). In chapter five, at the house of Jairus, 'He ordered (the people) strictly not to let anyone know about it' (5. 13), and so on. . . . Why is Christ so secretive? If he has done all these miracles and if they are designed to impress people, surely he would want to publicize them. But he tells people to be very quiet. Why the strange reserve about miracles, so entirely alien to our way of thinking about their purpose?

Alongside these demands for secrecy, there is another series of phrases in these chapters of St Mark to give us pause. In chapter six it is said about Nazareth: 'He could work no miracles there — he was amazed at their lack of faith' (6. 6). In chapter five, he says to the woman with the haemorrhage: 'My daughter, your faith has restored you to health' (5. 34). To Jairus whose daughter is dead he says: 'Don't be afraid, only have faith' (5. 36). In chapter two, 'Seeing their faith Jesus said to the paralytic . . .' (2. 2). In chapter eight the scribes say: 'We should like to see a sign', and our Lord replies: 'It's an evil and unfaithful generation that asks for a miracle' (8. 11).

Why this emphasis on faith? If miracles are meant to impress and astound, is not faith irrelevant?

We must look into these two problems in the hope that they will throw some light on the meaning of miracle.

Miracles played down

First, the secretive aspect. What is known as the 'messianic secret' emerges most clearly from St Mark's gospel. Very frequently the account of a miracle will finish with the demand that it be kept hushed up. Even other miracles which do not have that explicit command are still 'played down' by Christ. For instance the raising of Jairus's daughter has not only got the remark: 'Don't tell a soul', but before the thing happens. 'Oh! she's only asleep', and the crowds are kept out. It is almost as if Christ did not want people to realize the extraordinary thing that was about to happen. Certain cures he refuses to do in public; he draws the patient aside and does his work unobtrusively. Why? Some miracles he completely refuses to do even though circumstances would have guaranteed the maximum impact, for example before the influential scribes who asked for a sign from heaven, or before his fellow-townsmen in Nazareth who challenge him to do what he had done at Capernaum, or before Herod who is curious about this wonder-worker, or when his enemies challenge him to come down from the cross. What an opportunity to impress and astonish with a miracle! But he does not work one.

The same impression of secretiveness is conveyed by much of Christ's teaching. Whenever there is a suggestion that people are beginning to grasp that he is the Messiah he bids them not to say anything. He even seems to wrap up his explanation of the nature of the kingdom of God which he claims to bring, and speaks of it only in parables, offering the explanation only to his close friends. And it is only when he has that closed circle together with him far away from the crowd in northern Galilee that he opens up about his own mission. Why this secrecy and reserve? Didn't he want people to know?

Some scholars have suggested that this 'messianic secret' is not really our Lord's, but the evangelist's. St Mark particularly, like all the early Christians, was scandalized by the fact that his contemporaries had rejected Jesus as Messiah, and could explain the scandal away by pretending that Christ had kept his true identity quiet, and had explained it only to the apostles. But this answer unfortunately does not fit the facts. To preach a crucified Messiah is a ridiculously difficult thing to do if it is a sheer fairy story that he is the Messiah. The crucifixion itself would surely never have happened if Jesus had not somehow or other claimed to be Messiah and someone or other had recognized that claim.

No, the real answer is rather more complicated. This secrecy is not just a desperate solution thought up by the evangelits; it dates back to our Lord himself. He played down his messianic claim (in so far as he understood it himself) and his miracles because he had to. One has only to think of the kind of Messiah people were expecting to begin to understand. To people at large the word Messiah would conjure up a picture either of a political leader who would lead them in rebellion against the Romans, or of some super-conjurer who would get rid of the enemies by magic. If Jesus had come along and said quite openly, 'I am the Messiah', or if he had made himself known simply as a miracle-worker, he might have had a whole country behind him; but the work his Father had commissioned him to do would not have been done, because what he had to do was something more valuable than bring political independence, and something much harder to explain. The kingdom he was concerned with was something that would involve a whole life's work, and would not be understood fully until he himself had been through death and resurrection. That is why he is constantly saying: 'Don't tell anyone about this until the Son of Man is risen from the dead'. It is only slowly that men would be able to understand the mission entrusted to him by the Father. The full truth of what his work was could be seen only in retrospect — afterwards. So his whole approach is slow and very painstaking, to let his real mission dawn only very slowly on his audience. The suspense is not the evangelist's; it is Christ's own pedagogy, and it is forced on him by the very nature of his mission. There was a certain secrecy Christ exercised about his miracles, and it was out of fear of being misunderstood.

Well then, it may be asked, if he was going to be misunderstood, why did he do miracles at all? What is the purpose of the miracles?

Turning people into cabbages?

Perhaps we ourselves are responsible for this difficulty because of the rather shallow way in which we look at the miracles. Ninety-nine times out of a hundred we present Christ's miracles as if they were simply an apologetic proof of how true his message was. We quote his words: 'If you don't believe what I am saying, at least believe what I am doing — the works prove that I'm telling the truth' (Jn 10. 38); and there we stop, as if this is what the miracles are about. And this attitude suggests that whether Christ healed a man from leprosy or turned somebody into a cabbage it was all one and the same thing — this proof of his power, an apologetic argument that God had sent him.

I do not want to whittle down the apologetic value of the miracles, since Christ himself appealed to it in that quotation. But we ought to notice that he continued: 'so that you may come to know for sure that the Father is in me and I am in the Father'. That is to say, the miracles are not simply an apologetic proof of his message, but a proclamation of who he is. In fact when people ask him for miracles simply as a proof — merely for their apologetic value — he refuses to work them, as we have just seen.

So the miracles do have an apologetic value, but that is not their principal purpose. Principally the miracles are heralds of the kingdom, a proclamation of the fact that the kingdom has begun. The quotation we ought to have very much in our mind when we are thinking of miracles, is: 'If I by the finger of God cast out devils, cure diseases, raise the dead, then the kingdom of God is come among you' (Lk. 11. 20). In other words miracles are done not simply to back up Christ's teaching as if the teaching was something different from the miracles. The miracles illustrate the teaching; they're one and the same thing; they *are* his teaching. The miracles are not simply supporting something that he is saying in another context. The miracles are enacting in symbol what he is doing amongst us.

The miracles are not simply a guarantee that somehow or

other the kingdom is going to come; they are actually one of the means by which the kingdom is here and now present among people, happening before their eyes. All these marvels we read in the gospels: sight being given to the blind, lepers being cured, paralytics being healed, the deaf being given their hearing, the dead being raised from the dead, all these are symbols or signs pointing to the reality of what Christ the Son of God comes to do for us.

Nor is it sufficient to say that when he heals the body of someone, this is a picture of the healing that he is actually going to bring to people's souls. It is insufficient because Christ does not make that kind of distinction. He came to bring healing to the whole of man from the mortal blow with which mankind had been struck by sin. It was not only man's soul that was deprived of life by sin, but his body also. His body was condemned to death and all the sickness and disease which precede death. The kingdom of God is designed to overcome the rule of sin over mankind, and that rule has a stranglehold on us body and soul together. And so when Christ comes face to face with man he does not only, as it were, pardon, clean, heal his soul from sin, he cures all the sickness and the death that automatically goes with sin. When John the Baptist sends messengers to ask Jesus: 'Are you the one who is going to come, are you the Messiah?' he replies: 'Tell John what you are seeing; the blind are seeing, the lame are walking and the lepers are being cured' (Mt. 11. 6). This is evidence that the messianic age has come. The liberation of the whole of man from sickness and death is a concrete expression of the fact that the kingdom is here.

Each miracle, therefore, is a parable in action; each miracle is an epiphany of the Lord. In the miracle the kingdom of God is present and is active in our midst. The stilling of the storm, for example, is the first expression of the way that God's kingdom affects not only men's souls but the whole of nature which man's sin has thrown into discord. The exorcism of a demoniac is not just a wonder to make men gape, but a concrete replacing of the kingdom of Satan by the kingdom of God, a visible indication that Satan's hold on the world is being destroyed. With the demoniacs always asking: 'Is this kingdom come?' the answer each time is: 'yes'. The curing of diseases is not just a piece of magic, but the installing of the reign of God over the bodies and souls of men. The raising of the dead is not just the most striking wonder that Christ could perform — death is not just something more difficult to cope with than disease; it is the fullest expression of what sin does to men, it robs us of life; and when Christ tackles that, he is tackling sin in its last stronghold, and showing us in a concrete way the complete victory he is bringing from his Father to man as he is — body and soul.

This is precisely how the liturgy presents miracles to us when they are read out to us. When we listen to them at Mass we are not to think of them as a record of the way two thousand years ago Christ showed his power. They are meant to be here and now a symbol of what Christ is doing for you and me. He is continuing to do for us here and now what he did then, as he becomes present again amongst us. When people say: 'Why don't we see miracles happening today, except in odd, isolated cases in Lourdes, Fatima and so on?' the answer is: 'They do'. Exactly the same power is at work. If we don't believe this then we are not really Christians. The same Christ is acting and effecting the same powerful works of God in our midst in the sacraments.

Battered by thunderclaps?

That is why he so often demands faith, and refuses to work them when there is no faith present. Without the right dispositions a miracle of the kind described above would be quite useless. A divine conjuring trick, yes. This can be done for any audience; the fact that they did not believe would only urge the miracle-worker to do bigger and better tricks in order finally to force them to belief. But miracles are not like that. They are not done to save us the bother of thinking, of finding our way to God. They are not a thunderclap which batters us into saying yes when we wanted to say no. If we do not want to be impressed, then no amount of miracles will move us.

In other words the sincerity that a man brings to Christ is far more important than the wonder that happens before his eyes. To come and gape at a miracle just as something extraordinary and to follow Christ simply for this reason, is inacceptable to Christ. He demands faith; he demands that a person should commit himself completely into his hands, into what he is saying, what he is teaching — miracles or not — because without this attitude of faith, the miracle is not recognized. One simply does not see it for what it is, namely a herald of the kingdom, a decisive sign that the kingdom has come.

A blade of grass is a miracle

Let us try to sum up what miracles are, so that we know exactly what we are handling when we are seeing them in the classroom. What is a miracle? The classical definition is well known: a miracle is the suspension of a law of nature. This definition was based on a nineteenth century view of nature, as governed by fixed laws, and it suited the almost exclusively apologetic purpose for which miracles were turned to. God had fixed creation in a certain way; but when he wanted to show his presence he unfixed it! He interfered with it; he bent it to his own purposes so that his hand could clearly be seen.

Such a view of nature is out of sympathy not only with present thinking on what the world really is, but also with the Bible. In the Old Testament the word miracle does not occur; you find instead the 'mighty works of God', that is the wonders which signify and reveal God's presence. And of these mighty works, the greatest one is that which in the other view would reveal God least of all because it is so very normal — creation itself. For the Bible, this world that we see around us is not something ordinary which has to be interfered with before it can reveal God; on the contrary it is itself the most wonderful work of God. Every work of God is wonderful and reveals him, and for the man of the Old Testament a blade of grass is a miracle.

In this context we can understand that the Bible thinks of miracles not as objects, but as communications. They are one of the ways God speaks to us. That is why there is such a constant emphasis on faith. Without faith, without an openness to God, without a receptiveness and willingness, the miracles will not speak. We shall simply be deaf and blind to the communication of God.

These mighty works of God are very often referred to as the 'powerful works' of God. They exhibit God's power. The word power, however, does not here mean something unbeatable, irresistible. It is the power which we notice most deeply, because we are so weak and helpless ourselves. It is God's power to save us from our inability to save ourselves. And this saving power, which is present throughout God's working among us, comes to its climax in Christ, and specifically in the resurrection, which is the final embodiment of God's power to save those who commit themselves to him.

From this point of view it is interesting to see how often scripture speaks of the miracles just as it speaks of the resurrection, as something done not so much by Christ himself as by the Father, through Christ. Where we tend to speak of Christ rising from the dead, the New Testament speaks of the Father raising Christ from the dead. Christ is the instrument by which the Father saves us. Christ is the Word through whom God reveals himself to us. The normal scriptural way of referring to the resurrection is that the Father raised his Son.

And very frequently the miracles are described in the same way, as works done not by Christ but by the Father, who reveals himself to us through the activity of his Son and Word. The clearest example of this is to be seen in the story of the woman with a haemorrhage, where the miracle happens before Jesus is aware of it. The text says that he felt the power going out of him, and knew that something had happened (Mk 5:30). Unknown even to himself, he has been an instrument of the Father's power; the miracle has been worked by God in answer to this woman's faith, before God has even revealed it to his Son that he was the instrument of healing. This is worth pondering.

St John particularly is full of sayings of Christ which stress this aspect: 'I speak nothing on my account', Jesus says, 'only what the Father has revealed to me do I speak' (12:49), 'I speak only that which I have seen with my Father' (8:88), 'I do nothing of myself, only what the Father gives me to do' (8:28). Even the famous text where he asks people to believe not in himself but in the works that he is doing refers to those works as 'works that the Father does through me' (10:37).

It is the same saving power of God which is communicated through the apostles to the whole Church. It is only in that power that the Church is able to preach, to witness, to heal and to save. Miracles are simply part of that. When we see

them in this context I think we shall begin to see them for what
they truly are, no longer simply rather useful apologetic proofs,
but part and parcel of the vast saving power of God which is
illustrated in a blade of grass at one extreme and at the other
in the resurrection of our Lord Jesus Christ.

If we present miracles in that context, children might begin
to understand them. If we do not, then our telling of miracles
might do them more harm than good.

H. J. RICHARDS

The humanness of Christ

For many Catholics Jesus Christ seems remote and unreal, because they think of him as God or they imagine that somehow the God in him controlled the man in him, and so he cannot really be as fully human as any of us. This distortion of the truth has unfortunate results. Teenagers, for example, think him too remote from themselves; things were easy for him because he had divine powers, and they cannot take him as a model as they can some modern Christian hero. They feel that he is God in the guise of man, and therefore lacking in human understanding of their own situation and problems. Adults have practically the same ideas and feelings. As catechists, therefore, we should pay more attention than hitherto to Jesus' humanity; in doing so we shall contribute to overcoming the distortion just mentioned and we shall be in line with the Second Vatican Council which did not spend any time on the mysterious union of two natures in Christ, but did dwell time and again on the human condition of God's Son, who identified himself with men in their concrete condition. Let us give one quotation from among very many: 'By his incarnation the Son of God has united himself in some fashion with every man. He worked with human hands, he thought with a human mind, acted by human choice, and loved with a human heart'.

This quotation, from *The pastoral constitution on the Church in the modern world* (par. 22), is one which most Catholics accept in theory, but which, in actual fact, they do not seem to take quite seriously. At Mass we proclaim that Jesus Christ 'was incarnate of the Virgin Mary, by the power of the Holy Spirit, and was made man'. However, at the back of many minds is the idea that there is a catch in it; he couldn't have been an ordinary man because, of course, he was God. If we must believe that he was human, then the least we can do is to endow him with every conceivable virtue. This was the line taken by many spiritual writers, particularly in the nineteenth and early twentieth centuries; for instance 'That Christ was an

153

K

ideal man, a flawless personality of surpassing majesty and grace, can be denied only by such as do not want to see'.[1] Some do not even admit that he had human needs: 'He is not subject to the tyranny of sleep as we mortals are, who must pay the price of our mortality. With him, sleep is a gift freely bestowed, not a ransom paid by him. . . .'[2]

To understand why Christ has been divinized to the extent of concealing the man Jesus, it would be necessary to look at the first few centuries of Church history. Without going too deeply into the various disputes and heresies regarding Christ's person, we can see how these opinions developed. Some wanted to make Jesus simply a holy man who became divine. Others saw him as God who had borrowed a human form to come upon earth. The Church in her Councils had to make solemn pronouncements to preserve the fullness of the mystery. In stressing the truth that Christ was NOT just a man, over-emphasis came to be laid on his divinity. Although the extreme view of over-emphasized divinity, known as Monophysitism, has long been condemned, it does in fact persist to a very great degree in ordinary Catholic thinking, often in those who would be very distressed if they were accused of being heretics! It is reflected in devotional art, literature and hymns in many different ways. A number of people ask, sincerely, what difference does it make anyway as long as we try to live good lives? As a matter of fact it *does* make a difference, and a better understanding of Christ as a human person can give a greater richness to our own lives.

It is important to realize that the Incarnation cannot be completely understood. This fact, however, should not restrict efforts to deepen our present understanding. But it does mean that we keep firmly to the truth laid before us by the Council of Chalcedon, namely, that God and man are brought together in the person of Jesus Christ. Exactly *how* was not stated. If in this essay attention is being paid to Christ's humanity, it is not to down-grade his divinity or 'belittle' him. In actual fact, it is only when we fully accept that he was human, with all that this entails that we can begin to understand the wonder and depth

---

[1] *Christ is All,* J. Carr, 1928.
[2] *The Person of Jesus,* Fr James, O.F.M., 1942.

of God's love for us: 'His state was divine, yet he did not cling to his equality with God but abased himself to assume the condition of a slave, and being as all men are, he was humbler yet, even to accepting death, death on a cross' (Phil. 2: 5-8).

Some of those who find it hard to believe in the reality of Christ's human-ness, do so because of the notion that anything human, or 'of the flesh' is shameful. This word 'flesh' is generally used in a derogatory sense, but in its correct sense it is not something evil, only feeble, dependent, limited. Flesh (that is, man) in rebellion against God IS in a pitiful state, as there is nothing ahead except death. When Christ was made flesh, it was with all its accompanying weakness and frailty. In spite of this, he did not rebel, he was firm in his fidelity to his Father and he showed us what human nature is, in its fullness. Because of his triumph, he can now be described as 'one who has been tempted in every way that we are, though he is without sin' (Heb. 4: 15). Because of our sinfulness we cannot understand what the fullness of human nature should be, and even if we did understand, we would be powerless to attain it. It is only in Christ that our own humanity finds its meaning. C. S. Lewis shrewdly remarked: 'A man who gives in to temptation after five minutes doesn't know what it would have been like an hour later. . . . We never find out the strength of the evil impulse inside us until we try to fight it, and Christ, because he was the only one who never yielded to temptation, is also the only man who knows to the full what temptation means — the only complete realist'.[3]

We are told that by following Christ, we become more fully human. Conversely, by becoming more human, we become more Christ-like. The old kind of spirituality which led us to despise all things human seems to have missed the whole meaning of the Incarnation. To follow Christ we must deny ourselves not by despising our humanity, but by the effort and suffering which are essential in the striving after a fuller existence. Giving ourselves completely to a task, or a friendship, means trouble and pain — this is part of the crucifixion necessary before resurrection.

It is time now to look a little more closely at the human Christ as presented in the Council's words.

---

[3] *Christian Behaviour*, C. S. Lewis.

a) 'He worked with human hands'

Jesus was known as the son of Joseph, a carpenter. It was natural for him to have learned this trade, but it does not mean that the learning of it came necessarily easily to him. It is possible that he found no particular satisfaction in this work, and felt the frustrations many of us feel when faced with a job we don't like. His hands might have been clumsy, 'all thumbs', calling from him an extra effort and more concentration than if he had been a 'born' craftsman.

When he stretched out his hands to heal lepers, were they human hands, human flesh, open to contagion? Or were they miraculously safeguarded 'divine' hands? If the latter, then there is little room for inspiration on our part; but if not, there is a great encouragement to know he has truly shared our humanity.

b) 'He thought with a human mind'

This is the point which raises most difficulties. The Church has always taught that Christ had a consciousness of his divine sonship. This has often been taken to mean that he always knew who he was, and had no need to learn. 'Christ's human nature was immediately present to the Word through the hypostatic union. Since this union is an act of a spiritual being at its highest point, the reality of this union cannot be entirely unconscious. Christ was present to God because he was present to himself.' [4] However he could still need to acquire the knowledge only obtained through ordinary human means, and to gain his own experience of the world. For this reason we can hardly accept writings like this: 'What were the first thoughts of the divine infant, immediately after his conception? He offered himself and his whole life to the eternal Father as a holocaust, and a sacrifice for our sins. He said, in the inspired language of his prophet, "Behold I come".' [5]

It is now generally accepted that a baby's mind is a vast jumble of buzzing confusion, which gradually becomes more or less co-ordinated as time goes on. The child's development depends very much on the mother's attention; if she does not

[4] *Theology of Revelation,* Gabriel Moran, 1965.
[5] *Eternal Thoughts from Christ the Teacher,* Cardinal Cushing, 1962.

encourage him to explore the things around him, he may suffer later. He may become overreticent, or too impulsive. Overprotection can be as harmful as neglect. How much of this applies to Jesus? His mother certainly had the same task as any mother. She had to watch him fall and bang his head and scrape his knees until he learned to control his movements. Perhaps she listened to his shouts of frustration at not being able to reach some desired object. He had to learn, like any child, that he would be sick if he ate the soap, or its Palestinian equivalent. This is far removed from the image often proposed by spiritual writers; for instance: 'In the infancy, Mary had seen him, as it were, in still life, giving out heavenly mysteries, as the fountain throbs out water, with a seeming passiveness, though not unconsciously. . . .' [6]

As he grew to manhood, Christ's human development continued. He learned from the people, the things around him. He must have learned, at some time, from Mary or Joseph, that his conception had not taken place in the ordinary way. He learned from his study of the scriptures, from teachers and sermons. He didn't cease thinking with his human mind at any stage, even when conscious of his mission. He learned obedience through suffering, painful doubts, and prayer. He learned to obey through suffering. That he had to die a hard death himself became clear to him, and the details of that death would have been evident to him from what he had observed of the death of other criminals. He knew the grimness of suffering. When writers and artists make him out to be a sweet pious, 'up-in-the-clouds' being, they are robbing him, and the world, of something much deeper. 'In an age of concentration camps and atomic bombs, religious and artistic sincerity will certainly exclude all "prettiness" or shallow sentimentality. Sacred art cannot be cruel, but it must know how to be compassionate with the victim of cruelty, and one does not offer lollipops to a starving man in a totalitarian death-camp.' [7]

c) '. . . acted by human choice'

To be able to choose presupposes a necessary freedom. Jacques Maritain says that man is a free individual in personal

---

[6] *Under the Cross*, Fr Faber, 1903.
[7] *Disputed Questions. Sacred Art and the Spiritual Life*, T. Merton.

relationship with God. His 'supreme righteousness consists in voluntarily obeying the law of God'.[8] If Christ had known every detail, and possessed all knowledge of things past, present and future, his freedom would not exist. 'It is precisely in the unfolding of man's freedom that a certain lack of knowledge becomes necessary. If man knew everything to the last detail, whether present or future, his freedom would be paralysed.'[9] Karl Rahner also says that risk, 'the going out into the open, the trust in what cannot be foreseen, and therefore a definite kind of lacking knowledge, are necessary to the self-fulfilment of the person in the historic decision of his freedom'.[10] Christ chose to fulfil the will of his Father in all things, but in order to know it he had to have recourse to prayer and to study. He wasn't a kind of robot whose actions were all regulated by remote control, or previously programmed systems, although very often this is what he seems made out to be by spiritual writers. It is very difficult to correct this image. If we can put it right, we see the richness Christ's life offers to us. The greatest part of suffering in our own lives comes from our lack of knowledge of what is going to happen to us, or what is required of us. Our anxieties and worries come through fear of the unknown, more than from actual pain. Christ suffered intense physical pain, but this was not the wholeness of his crucifixion. In fact, many other men have undergone even worse physical torture.

There is far more to suffering than the merely physiological aspect. Christ chose to undergo all his sufferings, freely, but that did not make them any less severe. If he had lived in blissful union with the Father, his agony would have been much easier to bear, being only physical. This kind of description was and still is popular: 'The trembling of excessive pain passes over his sacred limbs, but does not dislodge the sweet expression from his eyes . . . now the cross is lifted from the ground with Jesus lying on it, the same sweet expression in his eyes. . . .'[11] Where is the agony expressed in Jesus' cry 'My God, my God, why have you forsaken me?' Christ was not an actor in a heart-

---

[8] *Education at the Crossroads,* Jacques Maritain, 1943.
[9] 'The Problem of Christ's Knowledge', Gutwenger; *Concilium,* Jan. 1966.
[10] Quoted in Gutwenger's article.
[11] *Under the Cross,* Fr Faber.

rending drama but a free human agent in the working out of our salvation.

d) '... and loved with a human heart'

A human being has feelings, emotions and needs which respond to love. He can also recognize these in others. Christ was lonely, weary, depressed and at times reduced to tears, for example at the death of his friend Lazarus. This was real, spontaneous grief, rising from his human heart. If he had divine knowledge that Lazarus was soon going to be alive again, why did he weep? 'On seeing Lazarus dead, he weeps. A God to weep! Yea, he weeps because he vouchsafes to weep; for he is the sovereign master. He commands every feeling as often as he wishes to experience them, and experiences them only when it is his will. . . .' [12] This again is unreal, not human. He almost seems to be able to 'turn on the tap' when he wishes to impress others; this does not increase our admiration or love. Christ wept because he was upset, because there was sorrow in the hearts of those around him, and he was able to share their grief. He entered into real relationships with those among whom he worked, and when anyone is prepared to have deep relationships suffering is to be expected. Because of his love of individuals, he was so much more open to being hurt than we are, who rarely have real, unselfish love. When someone we love deeply says something hurtful about us the pain is far greater than if a casual acquaintance had done the same thing, and it takes a longer time to heal.

Perhaps what has been said will be of help to catechists in making Jesus Christ a fully human person like the rest of us. As a final note might be added the need to stress that Christ today is fully human; if his humanness had ended with the ascension it would have little meaning for us in the twentieth century. The glorified Christ is a man now living on earth (as well as in heaven) in his new body, the Church; he lives in every human emotion, trial, worry, sorrow, as well as in every joy and satisfaction. He says to us, in modern terms, what he said to the apostles and first century crowds. When 'doing' the gospels, then, we might profitably use the expression 'Jesus says' rather than 'Jesus said'.

[12] *Last Retreat*, Ravignan, 1857.   SISTER EILEEN CARROLL

Penance
in the Primary School

Penance is an adult virtue which cannot be expected of infant and junior school children. As the proper religious and moral attitude to personal sin and sin in general, it is comprehensive and complex.

Penance has to do with sin. Now, it needs an adult mind really to grasp what is involved in sin, and in fact very few adult Catholics today have an adequate conception of sin. They will tell you it is a transgression of God's law. They fail to see that sin is a matter of man's love relationship with God; it is a refusal to love God and to love my neighbour in whom God is as it were incarnate. They have the further difficulty in grasping the fact that our relationship with God is known and manifested in our relationship with our neighbour. And it does not occur to them that a personal sin, perhaps a secret one, offends all the other members of the Church community. Yet these are three basic truths necessary for a proper understanding of sin. If it is so difficult for adults to acquire them, we cannot expect young children to understand sin.

Penance includes an honest acknowledgement of our sinfulness. Yet only an adult, having reached a certain maturity of mind and experience of life, can come to realize our human condition of sinfulness. Some children brought up in an environment of low moral standards may have the feeling that there is a lot of wickedness in the world, but they cannot realize that in every man, woman and child are the roots of evil ever ready to shoot up and spread. When we try to teach them the doctrine of original sin, we usually do more harm than good because they certainly misunderstand the mystery and draw damaging conclusions.

Only an adult can experience true repentance in the scriptural and theological sense. Under the influence of God the sinner looks at his present state of separation from God; he brings the past into the present in so far as it was a past sin which now causes him grief. Like the prodigal son, coming to his senses, he remembers the friendship he once enjoyed, detests the past sin, resolves to bring about a change in his life, to sin no more and to make amends. He knows by faith that his release from sin can come only from God and through Jesus Christ.

From this brief analysis it is clear that Christian repentance supposes a certain maturity of mind and strength of faith which are far beyond the capacity of young children.

Enough has been said to show that penance is an adult virtue. We can now go on to say that it is a permanent basic requirement in the life of a Christian. It is basic because of the reality of sin and sinfulness; not only does every adult fall short of the love he owes to God and his neighbour, but he runs the risk of destroying the relationship of love. It is a permanent requirement because the selfishness abiding in us will always be there to draw us away from loving God or our neighbour as we ought.

Because penance holds such an important place in our life, we should start early with children to lay the foundations upon which a religious understanding of it can later be built, and begin in the primary school the long slow process of fostering the spirit of penance. Without wasting time and effort on doctrine for which they are not ready, the teacher should take the children in their own concrete situations at home, at school and in the street to lay the foundations of penance. She herself will know where she wants to lead them, though she need not tell the children her goal and she will recognize that they will not reach that goal in their primary years. The goal or end result is the main component of Christian penance.

Let us consider some of the things which parents and teachers can do. Parents are, of course, far more important and influential than teachers, but as we are looking at school life we shall have teachers chiefly in mind.

1. *The teacher can prepare the way for the discovery of what sin is*

Let us trust that the teacher herself has shed that misconception of sin which is so widespread. If she thinks of sin as an objective act which is contrary to God's law, she is so incomplete as to transform sin into a forbidden action which automatically imposes superstitious guilt. Sin must be seen in terms of relationships with God, as a person's relation to God. Sin is a refusal to love God and our neighbour. Sin never exists as a merely objective action (stealing, missing Mass, etc.); there must be an involved person. Emphasis must be placed on the person and his love relationship to God and his neighbour. One must also reckon with the scope of personal freedom and consequent responsibility. If she bears this in mind the teacher will not reinforce that taboo morality which all children entertain: an action is wrong if it results in hurt or punishment. A child's misdemeanours — his naughtiness, his disobedience, lying, stealing — are not sins (except in an analogous sense) and should not be associated in the child's mind with the terrible evil that sin really is. The teacher, therefore, of infants and lower juniors may be recommended not to use the word 'sin' with her children. In this way, she will protect them from harmful guilt feelings and unnecessary fear. Expressions such as 'displeasing God our Father' or 'hurting those whom God loves' can be used; they are personal and imply a sense of relationship with God which we want to inculcate.

How does the good teacher guide the process towards the eventual discovery of what sin is? The whole tenor of her religious teaching is such that her children learn that God is our Father in heaven and we are children of God, our loving Father. Thus introduced to the idea of God the children instinctively imagine God in their parents' likeness. From the experience of parents' love they are enabled to perceive some image of God's love for them. A child's relationship with God follows the pattern of his relationship with his parents. If these are loving, then God appears as one who loves. If they are overstrict, irritable, easily angered, then God appears as a threatening person. Teachers are aware of a growing number of children coming from unhappy home backgrounds, but the presence of these unfortunates in the classroom does not prevent us from still speaking of our loving Father, because even the ill-treated children will understand that parents ought to be loving, kind, attentive and so on.

Together with the children the wise teacher looks at different aspects of home life and sees how we respond to the love of parents and others. She can choose from an endless variety of home situations and incidents, considering concrete examples of relationships with parents and other people: we listen to our parents, we speak to them, we show respect to them, we thank them for their goodness; we are kind to other children, help them, play with them, work with them, share with them.... In all this we are showing our love for parents and other people. At the same time we are pleasing God our Father in whose big family we all live as children.

It is important to note the procedure just outlined. We should start from the experience of the children, lead them to see what is the right thing to do, and to conclude that this is what God our Father expects of us. It is the opposite of what is too often done when teachers start off by telling us what God expects of us and then apply these rules to the children's situation. This latter method is bad theology and bad psychology. God does not first reveal his will and then we know what is right, and conclude that this is God's will for us. In other words, a thing is not right because God wills it; rather because a thing is right, God wills it. If we develop the habit of telling children that God wants them to do this, that and the other, they will think of God chiefly as an arbitrary lawgiver.

All through these years the teacher should introduce her children to the person of Jesus Christ: God's Son whom the Father sent to tell us how much he loves us. From the present point of view Jesus will be presented as one who loved God our Father very much, and other people. Jesus is also our big strong Brother who wants us to be big and strong like him. Again, in the talking about experiences in our own homes and at school, we find that to be like Jesus — loving God our Father and other people — means that sometimes we choose to do things we do not want to do and we choose not to do things we would like to do. Jesus was kind to people who hurt him, and he did not try to get his own back on people who hurt him. The difference between Jesus and us is that he always chose to do the right thing and so always pleased his Father, whereas it sometimes happens that we choose to do the wrong thing and displease our loving Father.

In this way the teacher will certainly be laying the right foundations for a true discovery and understanding of sin by

fostering an awareness of loving relationships on the human level
and on the Christian-religious level and drawing attention to our
occasional failures to love as we ought. She cannot force the pace
of moral development. Perhaps fairly early some children can come
to see their own misdeeds as a failure to love parents, brothers and
sisters, school companions, although psychologists warn us that
the taboo morality operates in children for much longer than
we think. In any case, the second stage, that of coming to see
that failure to love other people is a falling short in love for
God (a Person they cannot see) is a much more difficult and
slow process. We cannot fix an age when they can come to
realize it, largely because it will depend greatly on their Christian
upbringing at home. Do the parents themselves have a sense of
God? What is their attitude towards God? Do they relate the
daily life of the family to God? Do they develop their love-
relationship with God and let this be seen and absorbed by their
children? Is love for God and others the basis of their own
morality? Even in the best Christian families that true understanding of sin in reference to love comes slowly to children.

2. *The discovery of human sinfulness*

It has been said that a component of the spirit of penance
is a realization of human sinfulness. How soon can young
children begin to approach some inkling of this? From a reading
of religious psychologists it seems to be about the age of ten.
At this age they become aware, without being told by adults, of
their own little faults and feel guilty before God for things for
which they are not reproached by parents or teachers. They are
also aware of a certain dividedness within themselves, at least
to the extent of knowing that they could and should be better
in their behaviour and feelings towards other children. Then
again, they have noticed and are now talking among themselves
of the faults of adults, their teachers and parents. All these traits
are signs that they are beginning to perceive that we all have
some faults and failings.

With infants and lower juniors nothing need be done towards
fostering a sense of sinfulness. In fact, the teacher ought to go
against a tendency which starts young children on a wrong

line. In the past children have been given a list of blameworthy actions, for example lying, stealing, being disobedient, quarrelling and so on which are largely transgressions of parental norms without any reference to God, or else God is brought in as a means of pressure for the parents' convenience: 'you will make God sad if you do not do as I tell you'. The children are made to think they have committed sins and are sinful. This is most unfortunate. The children may be guilty of a wrong action, but they are not yet of an age to be morally accountable for their action. They cannot yet judge interior motives or intention. The wise teacher will explain why certain actions are wrong in order to help form the pre-moral conscience, but she will not call them sinful.

When talking about failings in our relations with others, the teacher should use 'we' and not 'you' which makes explicit that it is not only children who are at fault, but that adults also sometimes fall short in the love they should show to God and others. Then with the nine or ten year olds, when the term 'sin' has begun to be used and one speaks of the sacrament of penance, the teacher could well point out the significance of the fact that grown-ups, including priests and bishops, seek God's forgiveness in this sacrament. It is a simple concrete illustration, sufficient for the time being, to indicate that we are all sinful.

3. *Fostering repentance*

Repentance or contrition is the central act of penance. The teacher, remembering that a child learns to be sorry and to forgive not from formal instructions but from the experience of sorrow and forgiveness in daily life, can start to build up the attitude of repentance.

Plenty of opportunities arise to inculcate sorrow, because children are so very egoistic in their behaviour. The wise teacher chooses incidents in home and school life to help the children see that when they do wrong they spoil happiness.

By her handling of the frequent manifestations of selfishness in the classroom and playground she can bring home the notions of causing hurt, being sorry, making up, which will later constitute the Christian notions of offence, change of heart and amendment.

It is the same with forgiveness; experience comes long before any doctrine. Here I would stress most of all the forgiving attitude of parents and teachers. When a child owns up to having done something wrong and says that he is sorry, parents or teachers should forgive him fully. They may lay down some condition for the better behaviour of the child in the future, but they should genuinely forgive and forget the offence. In doing this, they are most closely reflecting the forgiveness of God, as so often portrayed in scripture.

In this way the child experiences human forgiveness in his daily life, and having had the experience he will come in time — probably before leaving primary school — to understand the loving forgiveness of God our Father. He finds that he has done wrong; he has expressed his sorrow to some one he knows and loves and he has been forgiven by some one he knows and loves. It becomes much more easy for him to understand a similar experience of forgiveness coming from the God he has been taught to know and love.

Besides being herself a model of forgiveness the teacher should encourage among the children themselves a spirit of mutual forgiveness.

From the experience of being forgiven they can learn to forgive others, a very important element in the Christian life, since we are taught to pray: 'Forgive us our sins as we forgive those who sin against us', and the parable of the unforgiving servant reminds us that forgiving others is a condition of God's forgiving us. So on the occasion of classroom squabbles and quarrels the teacher should encourage the children to forgive others and to show that they mean it by trying to be friendly with the person who hurts them.

4. *A community spirit of penance*

The teacher should prepare the way to a community spirit of penance, although she is aware it is not likely to be acquired until much later in life, if ever at all.

At about the age of nine when children feel the need to belong to some peer group, the teacher can develop the idea of community from the theme of friends. From these discussions she can enlarge their outlook to other communities: family, school, nation, Church. In all of them we have to learn to work agreeably and pleasantly with others.

Sin is seen as a breaking or a weakening of friendship, friendship with God, with Jesus, with others. We like to make up with our friends again. Well, Jesus knows this and provides a special way of doing so; this is the sacrament of penance.

5. *The sacrament of penance*

Nothing has been said so far about preparing children for the sacrament of penance. I will summarize some of the arguments for postponing first confession until the age of nine or ten.

(a) The sacrament of penance exists for the Christian who has deliberately turned away from God. The infant and junior child is incapable of such a turning away.

(b) A confession of devotion, the only one open to a child, is not necessary for him; and if on balance it is found to carry more disadvantages than advantages it had better be postponed until he experiences a need for it.

(c) The sacrament is not the only means of obtaining forgiveness of our offences. We should make use of other true forms of forgiveness within the Church, especially with children, until they can celebrate the sacrament with some meaning.

(d) The psychologists have shown that a child's mental powers develop very slowly and we cannot make him reason and form those moral judgments which make the sacrament of penance personally significant to him. Up to the age of nine or ten a child cannot help but see 'sin' as a taboo action, certainly not as a negative response to God's love.

(e) A child has great difficulty in expressing verbally what he feels guilty of; so he has recourse to reciting a list of faults put before him by teachers or parents, a practice he often keeps up for the rest of his life.

(f) A child attaches more importance to the mechanics of 'going to confession' than to being sorry and strengthening friendship with God.

(g) A child is incapable of understanding the real nature of sin and penance or the permanent character of repentance.

Some time ago the English bishops issued a report on introducing children to first confession and were generally in favour of confession before first Communion. They suggest two advantages of early confession. First, 'the sacrament of penance is not for them a necessary means of salvation, but it does remit subjective guilt and enables them to experience the loving care and mercy of God in a unique way'.

The sacrament is indeed a more formal and solemn way for the remission of sin, and for this reason can be reassuring to the child. But this advantage should be weighed against the possible disadvantages resulting from the more or less mechanical procedure of going to the sacrament.

The bishops also suggest another advantage. They say: 'At an early age (children) need guidance to help them recognize their faults, and this can best be given by the priest who is father and counsellor in the confessional'.

Teachers answer that this is just not true. Priests, with very few exceptions, are not competent to guide young children; they have not had the training. They do not know what goes on in the minds of children, they find it extremely difficult to speak in simple language intelligible to a child, and they tend to treat them as embryo-adults. The best people to guide children are the parents who know their own children intimately, and the teachers who work and play with them for five days a week.

6. *Preparation for first confession*

It will be reasonable to ask, on the supposition of postponing first confession, what preparation may be given to the child so that he celebrates the sacrament when its need is appreciated. I, therefore, offer some suggestions which the reader will find expanded in the booklets *Living in God's Family* edited by Fr P. Wetz.

With five and six year olds we do not talk about confession, and we need not use the word 'sin'. With them we strengthen the experience of love in home and school. The teacher should provide an atmosphere of *love, firmness* and *forgiveness*. Her love for the children, like that of the parents, is an image of God's love for them. Her love for them has tremendous religious significance; for having experienced this human love, the children can come to understand God's love for them and respond to it in their childish way. This experience of love is absolutely essential before anyone can come to any true discovery of sin.

The teacher's firmness in insisting on certain standards of behaviour in the classroom lets the children see that these are part of her care and concern for them. Prompt punishments for misdemeanours are accepted as just so long as the teacher does not show a nasty impatience.

Likewise, the teacher's forgiveness is an image of God's forgiveness. By showing a readiness to forgive and forget she helps the children to expect forgiveness from God.

In these infant years the teacher should explore with the children the communities to which they belong: the home family and the classroom family. In doing so she can lay the foundations for learning what it means to belong to God's family, the Church. In these communities we discover love, we share things, we sometimes quarrel, we are sorry for hurting others, we forgive others and are forgiven. . . .

The stories about Jesus will bring out his goodness, his care for others, his love for God his Father, and his love for us in what he did.

Along with these experiences and stories, the children will have songs, assemblies, hymns, activities, such as are found in Fr Peter Wetz's booklet *Confession at seven and ten*.

With seven year olds we can take the theme of '*caring*'. Through it we can get across the essential Christian attitudes of being kind, helpful, friendly, concerned for others. After this human experience the children will better understand how God our Father cares for us by providing for our needs because he loves us.

With eight year olds we can take the theme of '*sharing*', to foster the same basic attitudes of Christian living as in the year before. Sometimes we are selfish and do not share. Think about this. We spoil the love of home life, of school life. We do not like selfish people. We are sorry for having been selfish. We will put things right by sharing with others. In this year there can be a few non-sacramental 'services of penance' or 'assemblies'.

With nine year olds we can show the social aspect of penance by discussing friendship and communities.

L

In this same year teachers have found that non-sacramental celebrations of penance are a valuable way of fostering the spirit of penance. These celebrations may be placed at the end of a theme that has been treated, but should not be conducted as a revision of the lessons. A celebration is a religious experience carried out for its own sake, that is as a prayerful activity, as a turning into prayerful activity something the children have learned in the religion lessons. It does have a pedagogical value, somewhat in the manner of the liturgy which is dogma prayed and put into action. In the religious experience of a penance celebration the children experience the virtue of penance and thus, among other results, learn by doing.

Having built up the right attitudes over the years we shall have done the main work and need spend only a short time preparing the ten year olds for the first sacramental confession.

The teacher should use gospel incidents, for example the pharisee and the publican, the good thief, the lame man brought to Jesus, to show the fundamental attitudes of the penitent and the readiness of Jesus to forgive. Stories of the joy and the big change in the lives of Zaccheus and Mary Magdalen after they had received pardon will show the effects of the sacrament.

One can explain quite rapidly the mechanics of going to confession: the opening formula, the confessing of sins, listening to the priest, answering any questions, doing the penance. The emphasis, however, should not be on these externals, but upon the meeting with Jesus who brings us closer to God our Father.

The teacher should be careful what she says about what are traditionally called the necessary acts of the penitent. Thus, with regard to the examination of conscience the principle to remember is that the primary purpose of this self-searching is not to find particular sins to confess but to find grounds for sorrow and conversion. Consequently, it is unnecessary and mistaken to put into children's heads lists of possible sins. Priests know too well the bad habits which are acquired when this has been done.

Teachers will make no mistake about stressing the importance of contrition. They are advised not to insist on material integrity in the confessing of sins. The satisfaction will nearly always consist of a prayer; but the children should be told to listen carefully to what the priest says, because he might also tell them to perform some acts of kindness in the next few days.

It would be a good thing if the first confession were made a real celebration in which priests, parents, teachers and children take part. At present it is a somewhat fearsome ordeal in a dark confessional. But if we had some communal service during which the adults as well as the children make their confession, it would have at least two positive advantages: it would allow the children to identify themselves with the penitential practice of grown-ups, and allow them to understand that all of us, old and young, acknowledge that we are sinners but are confident of God's forgiveness.

F. SOMERVILLE

First Confession

It is a good thing that children's confessions are being re-examined in the spirit of renewal engendered by the second Vatican Council. We tell ourselves that the sacrament of penance is a most powerful factor in the religious development of us all, both adults and children; by means of it we are able to grow in experience of the living God who calls us to holiness and is ever ready to forgive us our sins. Yet in practice we are not so convinced of the alleged benefits, because our own experience and that of most of our acquaintances with whom we have discussed the matter do not seem to support the assertion. Perhaps, some people are now saying, the weakness lies in the first initiation into the sacrament, at least to a large extent, since early training produces life-long effects. In order to promote discussion there will be put forward here some difficulties of first confession as at present practised, then some objections to infant confessions, and finally some proposed changes on the pastoral level for the renewal of the sacrament in the life of Christians.

Difficulties

Those who prepare six or seven years old children for first confession and try to follow up the work done are well aware of the difficulties. It is enough simply to list some of them, in confidence that readers can verify them and add others.

1. A small child cannot commit serious sin, and yet he is taught the requirements of an adult confession.

2. An infant is only beginning to distinguish right and wrong, and in doing this he judges by the pleasure or displeasure of parents and teachers. He usually has a false sense of guilt or none at all. Teachers, for their part, generally accept as valid an outdated concept of the age of reason, and treat him as a miniature adult.

3. A child has great difficulty in expressing in words what he feels guilty of. So he repeats phrases from some list of sins in a book or as used by the teacher.

4. The child suffers anxiety. He is called to do something alone, at an age when he learns by doing things with others. He worries whether he will remember what to say and do in the confessional.

5. All children are afraid of darkness, and the little penitent has to go into the dark confessional. He becomes still more nervous if the voice behind the grille puts questions to him.

6. He is so drilled in the procedure of the sacrament (going into the box, saying the formulas, saying the penance, and so on) that he takes these mechanics to be the most important thing when going to confession, even though the teacher has stressed the necessity of sorrow.

7. In the follow-up priests and teachers foster regular confession by regimenting children and bringing them *en masse* to the church for confession, with all the defects of this system.

Objections to infant confessions

Although some of the difficulties could be removed by a more intelligent catechesis and reforms in confession procedure, others will remain precisely because children are children, immature and developing emotionally, mentally and socially. The problem, however, is more fundamental than that of improving present practice; objections can be levelled at the very fact of having infant confessions. Here are some criticisms made on grounds of religious pedagogy.

1. First confession before first Communion came in because it was considered the normal preparation for receiving the Holy Eucharist. Infant teachers took this preparation as their aim, and junior teachers widened the purpose of their work to helping children obtain the forgiveness of sins. One recognizes this fact in the language commonly used about cleansing the soul of stains, blotting out sins, making ourselves right with God. Leaving aside for the moment the misconceptions implied in this teaching, I consider that priests and teachers have been too short-sighted in their aim. What we should see our-

selves as really doing in the preparation of children for first
confession is trying to promote their sacramental life under
the guidance of the Spirit. The initiation needs to be placed in
a larger perspective. The life of a Christian is essentially a
sacramental life; consequently the aim of the religious educator
is to disclose the riches of the sacraments and set children on the
way of living the sacraments now and for the rest of their life.

2. Very many adult Catholics misunderstand the real nature
of sin, penance and a genuine Christian life. They think it
sufficient to keep on the right side of God's law, without ever
realizing that they are being continually called in the Holy
Spirit to ever greater holiness. The Council's chapter in *The
constitution on the Church* describing the universal call to
holiness would strike them as strange doctrine. Without exaggeration we could say that this mentality is a long range effect
of early first confession. When being prepared they were told
about sins and coached to examine their conscience according
to the ten commandments; they were to tell their sins to the
priest, say an 'act of contrition' and do the penance. They got
into the habit of mind whilst young that 'doing' this is the
sacrament of penance, and even though further precisions were
added in secondary school those first impressions and practices
persist through life. Priests are accustomed to hear adults
make their confessions as if they were still children. Not knowing better, many adults feel that these confessions are unhelpful
and they drop the practice altogether or else they go out of
routine and confess mechanically. This state of affairs may be
largely attributed to premature first confession.

3. In stressing so much the sacrament of penance for the
forgiveness of sins we have neglected the other means which
are at hand for the forgiveness of venial sins. Without wishing
to question the special value of confessions of devotion, a
number of pastoral-minded critics think that we should more
frequently remind adults of these other liturgical and extra-
liturgical means, and that we should definitely make use of
them with children until their first confession at the age of
nine or ten. In this way we should get rid of all the difficulties
of infant confessions and most of those experienced by and with
junior children.

4. The Church teaches that the primary right and duty of caring for the religious education of children lies with the parents. Priests and teachers recognize in theory this primary role of the parents. They also acknowledge that parents exercise by far the deepest and most lasting influence on their children, and that without the support of home background the finest efforts of a school are of little avail. In practice, however, where a Catholic school systems exists, the parents are left very much in the background when it comes to preparation for first confession. Sometimes the rights of the parents are ignored. Often the Church and school authorities leave the parents to think that the school takes over the chief responsibility for the children's religious education. All this is wrong religiously and psychologically. The priest should respect the wishes of those parents who want their child to go to first confession either sooner or later than the time arranged for the class as a whole. Efforts need to be made to involve all the parents in the work of preparation for the sacraments. Perhaps only few will respond with eagerness, but despite these possible disappointments both priests and teachers should try to make real what they admit in theory.

Here is a pastoral activity to be faced by priests and teachers. Priests could meet the parents and explain the religious significance of the sacrament as a sign of faith and a deepening of Church community life. They could also explain to them their responsibility in the religious education of their children, a thing which they may not have previously realized. Teachers are more likely to win the co-operation of parents if they put aside any appearance of superiority and make it quite clear that they regard themselves as helpers of the parents and want to help. Headmistresses of primary schools who have worked on these lines report that even nominal Catholics make an enthusiastic response. A series of short meetings are held in which parents are given a summary of the lessons given to the children in school; they are asked to help the child with home exercises and to pray with him and ideas are suggested for encouraging him to take up simple Christian practices. The best result of these meetings, says one headmistress, is the climate of sympathy between parent and teacher of which the child becomes very conscious, and this gives him a sense of security and satisfaction, two things necessary for spiritual development.[1] Further co-operation could perhaps be promoted if we looked around to see what others are doing. For example, we hear that the Dutch catechists have become convinced of the inefficiency of the old policy of trying to reach the parents through the children, and are now concentrating their efforts on the parents in order to reach the children.[2] Their leaders seem to be breaking away from the child-centred emphasis in the pastoral practices of previous generations in order to serve the adults who in turn serve the children.

5. A child's readiness for confession is very largely determined by the stage of development of conscience. Thanks to the studies of the psychologists we are becoming more convinced that with the over-simple understanding of the 'age of reason' being reached about the age of seven, infant confessions are fraught with dangers. The very uneven mental development of children points to a highly variable 'age of reason', moreover it is considered unwise to place first confession when one detects the first glimmerings of a moral conscience. The child still judges right and wrong too much through the approval or displeasure of parents for him to be capable of a personal conscience, and therefore of moral responsibility.

It is the task of all religious educators to help the child develop his conscience, a process which is slow, gradual and interior. Here again, we have been rather clumsy and superficial in our view of what conscience is. It is a much more complex reality than the power to judge the rightness or wrongness of a particular act of mine, as we used to be taught and is still repeated in moral manuals. Conscience is the experience of responsibility in the exercise of freedom. God made men with the gift of freedom. A person has the power to realize himself as a person, to become as fully a man as he possibly can, by the choices he makes in the concrete circumstances of his life. Along with freedom goes responsibility. This responsibility means more than that he is held accountable for his actions; it means also that in his actions he responds to the moral

---

[1] Sister John, S.N.D. 'Co-operation between Home and School in Religious Education', *The Clergy Review*, Nov. 1966.
[2] See *Fundamentals and Programmes of a New Catechesis*, pp. 248-252. Duquesne University Press.

demands he discovers in his present situation. Now the Christian, possessing as he does the light of faith, knows that he is related to God, his Creator and Father, and also to his fellowmen with whom he is to live in right relations. Developing my conscience as a Christian means, then, becoming the kind of person God wants me to be; it means responding in the choices I make to the law of Christ, to the law of my nature, and to the inspirations of the Holy Spirit who makes known to me the demands of the two-fold law of love in my present concrete situation.

Clearly, the nature of conscience calls for a postponement of first confession after the age of six or seven. Time is required for the child really to experience responsibility in the exercise of freedom and to learn how to judge with love of God and his neighbour as criterion. Religious educators, in helping to awaken and develop a child's conscience, must proceed by slow stages from babyhood onwards. First and foremost, they need to inculcate a deep awareness of God as our loving Father who calls us to love him, and also the conviction that after the example of and with the help of Jesus our Brother, we love God by loving our fellows who like ourselves belong to the family of God. Then by stages one trains children to a sense of sin. When one realizes the tact and patience required to help this inner growth of conscience, one understands the objection to infant confessions.

6. The essential element of the sacrament of penance is repentance in the biblical sense of the word. It is a big change in a man's whole being giving a new direction to his life. It is also a continuous process which is to abide in the Christian. Having taken the first step, he must go the whole way, leaving his former self-centredness and putting himself progressively more and more under the rule of God. Yet as he belongs to a sinful world, he is weak in his fidelity to the basic orientation of his life. He has a tendency to be offensive in his relation to God and neighbour; and so he needs to cultivate a spirit of repentance.

A training to repentance can well be started early with the pre-school child. At home the parents by their own example and with gentle patient firmness can persuade their child to good behaviour and right attitudes and lead him to discover and be sorry for his faults and feelings. The discovery is important because without the experience of having done wrong he cannot have repentance. In the infant school the teacher does the same, without introducing notions which the child cannot understand, such as the ten commandments. The word sin need not be used yet, because these children cannot understand the crucial significance of personal decision for any sin, and if a teacher talks about sin she might provoke harmful guilt feelings.

Both at home and at school the earliest initiation into repentance should be made without explicit reference to God. The children should be induced to sorrow and resolve because the misdemeanour is against right order, against the love or obedience we ought to show to others. The reason for saying this is that we can build safely only upon the basic daily experience of the children. If we tell a small child his action is wrong because God forbids it, he will probably think that God is simply a lawmaker, whereas if we explain its wrongness on the human level he will come in time to make the connection with what our Father in heaven expects from his children. Moreover, we ourselves should remember that an action is not right or wrong because God commands or forbids it; God does not impose his will on reality from outside, but reality expresses his will; because a certain behaviour is good, God wills it.

7. The sacrament of penance has long been a very private, even secretive affair between penitent, priest and God. But we are becoming more aware of its ecclesial dimension and the social character of sin and pardon. Theologians are saying that there is no such thing as a private sin; a man's sin affects the whole community; for if one man fails to contribute his part to the life of the whole Body, he contracts out of the social implications of his baptism and the whole Church is weakened. Then again, whilst we have hitherto described sin as an offence against God, they are now stressing that it is also an offence against one's neighbour, a refusal to love one's neighbour as one should. Love of God and love of neighbour are indivisible — sin is an offence against our neighbour. Consequently, because sin is an offence within and against the Church, its forgiveness must come from the Church. The early Christians realized this fact more profoundly than we do; for the Church

authorities instituted the rite of public reconciliation of the sinner. A relic of the social character of pardon is found in the rite of the sacrament today: in the absolution the sinner is first reconciled to the Church and thereby reconciled to God.

This social aspect of the sacrament has to be brought home to Christians. The only way to start is by practising mutual forgiveness within the family circle. Children can be trained to ask forgiveness of parents after being naughty, and in their turn to forgive brothers and sisters who break their toys and so on. Likewise at school, when infants and juniors hurt each other, as they often do, they can be taught to practise forgiveness among themselves.

Up to the age of nine children do not seem capable of a social sense; but at this age they become group conscious, they begin to gather in gangs, and the code or rules of the group play a big part in the setting of norms by youngsters for their own behaviour. The teacher can make use of this group experience to inculcate the community aspect of sin and pardon. In addition one can discuss with these pupils why we say the 'I confess' at the beginning of Mass: we publicly acknowledge to God and to each other that we have done wrong and want to be forgiven.

Changes proposed

Because faulty religious practices acquired in early childhood become extremely difficult, if not impossible, to correct in later life, some changes on the pastoral level are desirable for the preparation of children for first confession. In the laying of these foundations it is wise to adopt a policy of *festina lente,* make haste slowly. The first confession will be profitably delayed until the age of nine or ten when the child can begin to understand the significance of sin with which he will become acquainted in adult life, a complete turning away from God or an offensiveness against God and neighbour; when he can also begin to appreciate the meaning of repentance and the ecclesial dimension of the sacrament.

Until this first celebration of the sacrament the children would make use of the various means which the Church teaches are available to all for the forgiveness of venial sins. In particular

we could give value to the gospel precept of asking forgiveness
of one another: 'If you are offering your gift at the altar, and
there remember that your brother has something against you,
leave your gift there before the altar and go; first be reconciled
to your brother, and then come and offer your gift' (Matt. 5:24).
Are catechists themselves sufficiently convinced that pardon
extended by parents to children, teachers to pupils, by one child
to another is a true pardon in Christ?

The parents should be brought much more into the fore-
ground than hitherto. Teachers tend to be critical of parents
and fear they may cause disruption of school arrangements.
Yet teachers are helpers of the parents in the matter of religious
education. Fortunately, it so happens that parents do visit
primary schools regularly for medical and dental inspections;
so it is fairly easy to make direct contact with them and promote co-operation. Parents, not priest or teachers, are the best
judges of the awakening of personal conscience in their child
and of his readiness for confession. Their wishes are to be
respected regarding the time of his first confession.

In the years between first Communion and first confession
the initiation into this latter sacrament will be mainly through
celebrations in the classroom or church (among more fervent
families in France and Belgium they are also held in the home).
These celebrations are short religious services in which a truth
or attitude related to penance is prayed and lived, more than
explained and taught. In fact, a well devised service does not
call for explanation; it is self-explanatory. It is conducted in
an atmosphere favourable to the living activity of faith by the
whole person, mind, heart and will.

Some practitioners speak of penitential services and keep to
themes connected with penance, for example sorrows, sinfulness,
pardon. They undoubtedly contribute to developing insights and
attitudes to penance. The Dutch, it seems, prefer a wider context.
They work out celebrations of Bible themes or events on the
occasion of Mass-going and especially of big feasts in the
liturgical year.

The Dutch have also introduced a communual celebration
of confession prior to private auricular confession. At first
there is only a general confession that the children make together. They examine their behaviour as Christians whilst

priest or teacher suggests possible faults of selfishness. They ask pardon of God, of their parents, of their peers. This is followed by a general absolution. At a later stage, nine or ten years old, they celebrate communally as before, but those who wish to make an individual confession are invited to confess privately at the end of the common celebration. (I leave it to the pundits to discuss whether the general absolution is a sacramental one; the main thing, the forgiveness of sins, is obtained.) Thus the transition from public celebration of confession to private confession is made when the child shows a desire or feels a need for it.

In the year in which the children will celebrate the sacrament for the first time, one should give a direct preparation for the sacrament itself. The main work will already have been done during the previous three or four years during which right attitudes will have been acquired. Now the catechist will not need much time to prepare the children for a confession based on true repentance and with thought to the community aspect of the sacrament. The sacrament should be presented not as a cleansing of the soul but as a meeting with Christ and the People of God at which he brings us the Father's forgiveness and strengthens us to resist evil. The first confession is a beginning of regular meetings of this kind. In this way confessions of devotion are in no way undermined, but, being started at an opportune stage of moral and religious development, are enhanced in esteem, and the special benefits deriving from them are likely to be more effective, since the penitents have been trained in a way that is opposed to routine mechanical confessions.

C. G. ARMSTRONG

Teaching original sin

Teachers are aware that the doctrine of original sin as it has long been presented bristles with difficulties and theologians today are very dissatisfied with it. But teachers themselves are in a more awkward situation than the theologians, because when they are giving the traditional teaching they know that the pupils raise difficulties and objections which cannot be answered, and that they carry away from school for the rest of their lives the painful impression of some unfairness or injustice on God's part since we are deprived of grace because of a sin some one committed thousands of years ago.

Fortunately, some radical re-thinking of the notion of original sin has been going on for a number of years, and although the modern view is not yet worked out in all its details, we have enough to enable teachers to avoid the former pitfalls and to give a sound teaching which safeguards the ancient dogma of man's fallenness and God's redemption. The re-thinking is due not so much to dissatisfaction with the old presentation as to the impact of recent critical scriptural study and of the new scientific world-picture since Darwin. I do not intend to discuss the matter theologically, but rather to offer some teaching suggestions that follow from the accepted findings of the theologians.

It is advisable that the teacher avoid the term 'original sin' as much as possible, because it is equivocal in sense (Adam's sin and the sin we inherit) and because of its associations: a first couple Adam and Eve, their sin of disobedience, a serpent, something that happened once at the beginning of the human race.... It conjures up a whole series of mistaken notions. Consequently, never use it in the primary school. In the secondary school we can teach its reality without using the term itself until Form 5 or 6. We can use instead 'mankind's sin' or the 'sin of the world'. In this way we make it known that original sin belongs to contemporary history, not simply to the origins of the human race.

When giving the formal lessons on original sin we should take care to treat it in its right context which allows us to keep a proper perspective. Of course, throughout all religious teaching the main truth of the dogma, namely that all men are sinners and saved, will be implicitly present. But when we come to treat original sin specifically, we should place it in its Christian context, that is along with the teaching about Christ as the second Adam. It is a mistake to follow the old practice of treating it early in a religion course after the lessons on creation, as you find in most manuals. When we tackle the subject immediately after creation we give original sin too little and too great importance. Too little, because the story appears to the pupils as a sad sequel to the wonderful work of God's creating the universe and man and we fail to show man's fallenness as a present-day fact. Too great importance, because it appears to the pupils as an early failure in God's plan for mankind and that from almost the beginning of the human race he has been spending his time repairing that early breakdown.

For doctrinal and pedagogical reasons, therefore, we do much better to place the lessons on original sin after those on Christ's resurrection. One can teach the doctrine of original sin with any semblance of completeness only when one has seen the significance of Christ's paschal victory, which alone puts original sin in its true perspective: man sins and God saves; he saves him through Christ. This statement is true of Old Testament times as well, because even then God was saviour of his people with a view to Christ who was already present to the world though he was not yet become flesh (Col. 1. 15-17).

A further practical suggestion is that in teaching the doctrine of mankind's sin we should observe the sound pedagogical principle of working from the known to the less known. We have not been doing this. We used to start in the obscurity of dim pre-history about which we know nothing. We took the Genesis myth as narrating a historical fall of man, whereas the biblical writers were no wiser than we are about what actually happened. A much better procedure is to start from the facts of daily life today and try to understand them in the light of Christian experience through the centuries and of what is now known about human origins. Christianity does not depend on belief in an actual historical fall. It depends on belief in a holy and loving God who created a world that is fundamentally good; yet we live in a world infected by evil which has penetrated the lives of men. In God's good world how is this to be explained?

So the stages in the lessons I suggest might be as follows: (1) the fact of evil in the world around us today, (2) the fact of evil in ourselves, (3) how to account for this sin situation.

The classic presentation of the doctrine has taken such deep root among Catholic adults that a new one brings alarm to them. Young Catholics are more open to new ideas, but they suffer hang-overs from what they have heard or read of the earlier thinking. Consequently, there are certain views which the teacher must stress in order to clarify the doctrine and to show that the new presentation does not conflict with the Church's faith.

First, the early chapters of Genesis are a pictorial representation of theological truths. They are not to be taken literally. Yet most Catholics still hold a more or less fundamentalist interpretation of these chapters and accept all the words uncritically. As a result they assume positions which are no longer supportable, and if they are our pupils they ask questions which need not arise: for example were not Adam and Eve endowed with magnificent qualities (preternatural gifts) before the fall? did they not live in an earthly paradise? what was the nature of their sin? what about the serpent? why should their sin be handed on to us? is it fair? how can sin be handed on by physical generation? These false yet real difficulties would be avoided if we insisted that the Genesis story is a myth; the writers, wishing to teach religious truths, had to express them in a concrete pictorial way as was customary in folklore. So we have to separate the religious truth from the dress in which it has been garbed.

Secondly, many Catholics imagine that they have to believe that Adam and Eve were real individuals. They think that they are the first man and woman from whom we are all descended, and that unless we hold this view it is not clear how some other doctrines of the Church can be reconciled. Yet scientists say it is much more probable that the human race has evolved from a group of couples. We should point out to pupils that the dogma of original sin is compatible with either monogenism (one couple only at the origin of mankind) or polygenism (a plurality of couples evolving more or less simultaneously and independently at the origin of mankind). Remind the pupils that the word 'Adam' used in Genesis is a collective noun meaning 'man', the human race, rather than a proper name of an individual.

Thirdly, stress the unity or community of mankind. The dogma is not about Adam and Eve in the garden of Eden, but about mankind's estrangement from communion with God and its restoration. I have mentioned the uneasy suspicion of unfairness or injustice in God for making us suffer the consequences of something committed by an ancestor ages ago. This difficulty would not arise if we were convinced of the unity of the human race and its community in sin. All men form a unity. We are all one with men of the past, present and future, having a common origin, common nature and common destiny. We are all persons. And being a person means being related to others; we all form one complex network of mutual relationships, one community of inter-related giving and receiving. Each one of us is affected in thought and action for good or ill by our environment, a phenomenon which has been brought to still clearer notice by the social psychologists.

Presentation in the classroom

It would be wiser not to teach the doctrine of original sin at all in primary school. The teacher is sure to do far more harm than good if she tries. Unfortunately, we still find syllabuses setting down this 'sad story' to be told to infants and juniors, and thus perpetuating the false ideas which will probably never be shaken off. I would go further than discourage lessons, and advise the teacher never to use the expression 'original sin'. The children may have come across it in books or at home, but let it not come from their teacher; if she has to refer to the notion at all, she can say men's sin. If the children do ask questions about Adam and Eve and the serpent, just say that it is a story invented by people hundreds of years ago to tell that men have committed sin since the beginning.

In Forms 1 and 2 of secondary school it is still too early to approach the subject through the Genesis story; it would remove for the pupils this Christian doctrine from the world of reality. Nowadays these children study themes: about themselves and the various communties to which they belong, for example the family, the local parish where they were baptized and the family of the Church. Regarding themselves they now realize that, besides having good qualities, they do things which they know are wrong, they want to do things which are sins, and they are often pulled between doing good and doing evil. Regarding the family they grow in the conviction that it is the place where they find protection, food and love. Similarly, the family of the Church which we enter at baptism, can be, with all the helps it offers us, a place of protection, strength and love helping us to overcome the evil in the world.

In Forms 3 and 4 the pupils study personal relationships. In the course of it they can study the various groups to which they belong, for instance family, school, town, country. These various community environments have effects upon us in our development as persons. For the members of the groups to develop right relationships, we need certain qualities, trust, openness, thoughtfulness for others, generosity, self-forgetfulness and so on. Yet when we look at even the best examples of group living we find an inherent weakness resulting in misunderstandings, disharmony, oppositions, alienations and the rest. Something must have gone wrong in our human condition since we all have a propensity to disrupt those relationships in which alone we become fully human.

If we look at Jesus in his relationships with others we find he was 'a man for others' because he was in the first place a man for God. In his relationships with others he accepted people just as they were at the moment and treated them as persons. People, for their part, realizing his respect for them, opened themselves to him in personal relationships. Many gospel stories illustrate Jesus' being for others, for example Nicodemus, the Samaritan woman, Zacchaeus, Mary Magdalen, the apostles. . . . He appears as the one who 'brings together into one body all the scattered children of God' (Jn 11. 52). The Church, the Christian community, is the continued presence of Christ on earth. The Christian community is and should be seen as the place which helps men to overcome their inherent weakness (their sinful condition) and to live in harmony.

In Forms 5 or 6 any theme involving the study of man can introduce the doctrine of the sin of the world. At some point, as every teacher knows, the question of evil arises. Let the pupils bring up examples of evil which they know. They will quote numerous examples of physical and moral evils. Sort these out. Do not give much prominence to physical evils which are nobody's fault, earthquakes, sickness and so on, since they are the result of the action and reaction of the forces of nature.

Let the pupils see that the evils which chiefly disturb us are those which men inflict upon their fellowmen: wars, oppression, murder, theft, cruelty and so on. Whence do these arise? From men's injustice, aggression, hatred, jealousy, prejudice and so on. The point of bringing this out is to show that sin comes from within men.

Discuss how these evils could be done away with. This would take place only if men showed mutual love, trust, justice, generosity, openness, thoughtfulness and so on. The point of this is to be able to show that Christ possessed these qualities, preached them, and communicates them through his Spirit to his followers so that they may overcome the evil in the world.

Having seen the fact of wickedness all around us, we are now ready to acknowledge that we ourselves are no exceptions. Discuss the fact of evil in ourselves: we do harm to others; we are conscious of a dividedness within ourselves between good and evil and only too often we choose to do evil. The point of this discussion is to lead to the inescapable conclusion that we are *all* involved in sin. All mankind lives in a sinful situation. We are born into a sin-situation. We can speak of mankind's community or solidarity in sin.

The next step is to discuss how we are to account for this sinful situation in which we are all involved. Note how at all times in history men have asked themselves: why is there so much evil in the world? Draw upon ancient and modern poets, dramatists and novelists. This perpetual question indicates that evil has been always and everywhere present in the world.

Then we go on to say that Christians claim to have an

answer to this question. Their answer is based upon what God has revealed in the scriptures, especially the writings of St Paul.

The teacher may feel inadequate to give the full teaching of St Paul. This does not matter. He can keep to a commentary on Romans 5. 12-21, the passage on which the Church bases her doctrine.

The general argument of Paul here is: Jesus Christ by his death and resurrection has saved *all* mankind from sin; therefore, if all mankind is saved, all mankind must have sinned. More particularly, St Paul, looking at the world of his own day, saw that all men were sinful and incapable of freeing themselves from this condition. But Paul was far from pessimistic, because he knew and taught that although sin was strong and universal, God in Jesus Christ had conquered sin and had given men the means to overcome it. Jesus Christ had conquered the sin of the world, and he is the representative man, the representative of the whole human race; consequently, although mankind's sin continues to have a hold upon men, that is evil persists in the world, it does not have the mastery nor will it have the last word. Good has triumphed over evil, good is now stronger than evil despite appearances, and good will prevail in the future.

This is the main message of St Paul; it is a good news. But it does not answer the question of how sin arose in the first place. In his own thinking of the origin of sin, Paul the Jew was naturally influenced by the Hebrew scriptures with their story of the fall of man as told in the book of Genesis. At this point the teacher can give a critical account of the Genesis myth, a story not to be taken literally but used to get across a religious truth. He can consult some recent exegesis of Genesis 2 and 3, for example, the one in *The Theology of Original Sin* by E. Yarnold SJ.

Throughout the teaching at this age it is better to give preference to the expression 'the sin of the world' for 'mankind's sin' without totally excluding 'original sin'. We should make it known that we are treating a truth that belongs to contemporary history rather than to the origins of the human race. The 'fall' of man takes place every day. The weight of evil burdens every man as he comes into the world. He is born into a sin-situation of mankind and lives in it. In baptism Jesus Christ gives us entry into the Spirit-filled community, the Church, in which we are freed from the estrangement from God and in which we find the means to overcome the world of sin. We continue to live in a sinful world and so still have to struggle to preserve the freedom that belongs to the children of God.

Such a presentation combines the best of biblical exegesis and modern evolutionary evidence.

F. SOMERVILLE

Re-thinking on prayer

Things are not what they used to be. Lay people are seeing that time-honoured devotions like benediction, novenas, *bona mors* and the rest are fading out. Popular prayers like the rosary, litanies, *Hail holy queen* and so on seem to be on the decline. The new Mass is, for many of them regrettably, no longer a service where reverence and silence dominated and you could get on with your private prayers. Teachers are noting that teenagers show an aversion to the formal prayers at the beginning and end of class. Older Catholics are understandably puzzled. What is happening? Are we Catholics losing our sense of prayer? Are the Church powers that be changing our old religion? They are concerned. They instinctively feel that prayer is the barometer of faith. If their children are not being taught the prayer forms which have nourished generations of Catholics and if their children are opposed to the formalism of conventional attitudes they are anxiously wondering whether the rising generation is ceasing to pray.

More significant still, one hears on all sides of priests dropping the recitation of divine office and of religious being slack about the practice of morning meditation. They find some way of justifying their behaviour, but feel uneasy about the validity of their arguments.

On the other hand, one cannot help but notice another phenomenon. Not only Catholics, but other Christians as well, especially the young, are seeking new forms of prayer that are free from the formalism of conventional attitudes and old formulas. I am thinking particularly of the growth of diverse prayer groups, of which those connected with the Jesus movement and the Pentecostals are only two examples among many. These young people want to pray rather than say prayers. They are often members of a church, but they find the institutionalism of their church cramping and abhorrent; so they meet together elsewhere in small groups and share their reflections on the gospels. Sharing seems to be the basic characteristic.

A quiet revolution is taking place in the attitudes to prayer, a matter of such deep importance for the Christian life that the various changes are obliging anxious pastors and thoughtful laity to re-think the traditional ideas of prayers.

The changes are due, I think, to a combination of sociological, psychological and theological factors. It is a complex problem; these few pages will confine themselves to some of the theological factors at work.

A widened concept of person

Whatever one may wish to say about prayer, one must start from some essential presuppositions. One of these is that prayer is a realization of our relationship with God. To grasp the nature of prayer, therefore, we need to understand something of the two terms of the relationship, God and the man who prays. Both terms, however, are elusive to some extent, since both are a mystery. In recent years theologians have been re-thinking both terms, and the result has had repercussions on the understanding of prayer.

Who prays? Albert prays. Elsie prays. What is Albert or Elsie? We have stopped answering that man is a rational animal, because he is more than an animal and only too often irrational. We are also ceasing, after many centuries, to hold a dualism in man of separate soul and body. We no longer glibly say he is a composite of body and soul. Under the old view we used to imagine that it was the soul part which did the praying. Recall the stock phrases: prayer is 'the soul's communing with God', 'the language of the soul', 'the breathing of the soul'; a prayer-book was a 'garden of the soul'.

Albert prays. And Albert is not a soul. He is a chap living in a particular neighbourhood and in relationship with a particular family, certain friends and acquaintances. Albert is a whole complex of body, mind, will, imagination, physical strength and weaknesses, feelings and emotions, a bundle of contradictions, tensions, illusions and aspirations, an incomplete self with hopes of completion, a network of relationships in which he is strengthened and weakened, liked and disliked, encouraged and frustrated. He is his past, present and future, all in one. All he has been and done since birth has made him the sort of person he is now. All those past experiences in childhood, at school, at work, at recreation, are influencing him today and the way he now looks at life. The future also is exercising its influence on him to the extent that what he wants to do and become in the future is determining the choices he makes today.

This very mixed-up evolving creature is the real man who prays. Albert brings that whole caboodle to his prayer; he cannot leave aside any of these characteristics when he prays. It was the weakness of the older spiritual writers that they did not take this realistic view of the real man in his life of prayer. One can sympathize with the housewives who reacted to the unrealistic assumptions of a priest writer in *The Tablet* a few months ago when they reminded him that a married woman has to pray with the children screaming round her or when her crippled mother-in-law is driving her mad with constant requests. It is rather ludicrous when spiritual writers and preachers advise people in family life to set aside so many minutes for quiet prayer in a private room of the house. With children around there is no private room and their whole time is taken up with the problems and drudgery of daily life.

If, however, we take the wider view of man at prayer, a complex creature building his future from his past, living together with other persons, and confronted with the varied challenges of life, we must come to a broader understanding of prayer. It is bound also to influence the way a man prays.

Changing ideas of God

Prayer is to God, or it is not prayer at all. It is the human response to God's approach. Yet God is a much greater mystery than man. Although the one true God is always the same, men's ideas of him change with changes in culture, and this fact will have effects upon their attitude in prayer.

When most Christians held a two-world view — as some still do — many used to think of God somewhere outside and beyond this world in which we live. His transcendence or otherness was predominant in their minds. When they prayed 'Our Father who art in heaven', they imagined him dwelling in some place far from this world.

Admittedly this assertion needs some qualification, because these Christians did not think of him as entirely removed from this world; they also thought of him somehow present to this world and acting upon it, for example guiding events, creating each soul, working an occasional miracle, and sometimes coming to our aid in answer to prayer. He was, it would seem, present to the world, but present *alongside* men, somewhat after the manner of an omnipotent 'fellow-worker' whose presence we acknowledge but with whom there is no truly personal union.

In contrast to that distance of God which was uppermost in people's minds, theologians nowadays are putting due emphasis on God's immanence and nearness. God is Creator. Creation is a continuous activity of God. He makes the world *exist*. All things are totally and continuously dependent on him. In him they live and move and have their being. God is seen to be the ground and source of all that exists. His creative and sustaining presence is to be found everywhere. God is not just alongside men, he is within them. God is transcendently immanent in the world.

Moreover, God is the *personal* ground of all being. Words like ground, source, force are abysmally misleading if they hinder us from seeing God as a Father who loves and freely communicates with his human creatures. His union with them is a truly personal one, more close than that between parent and child or husband and wife. God is present and active within men, dynamically letting them be and enabling them to become freely their true selves.

The implications of these insufficiently appreciated truths make a big difference to our understanding and practice of prayer. God is in this world of ours and nowhere else. As creator and sustainer he is involved in everything that happens. Nothing is outside his attention, care and concern. He is creatively present at the very centre of human experience: in things, in events, and especially in men, without forgetting he is fleshed in the man Jesus Christ.

Our prayer consists, then, in being conscious of God living in and for this world. Since we encounter him only where he is, namely in ourselves, in our fellowmen and in the events of daily life, it is there and only there that we can listen to him and respond to him in prayer.

Different language and the same reality

One notices that the old familiar terminology is being less used, though the reality for which the terms stood is retained.

Prayer is traditionally described as a raising of the mind and heart to God. As far as we know this description is still found satisfactory and there is no desire to drop it. However, theologians do point out that we are here using analogical language. Can we raise up our minds with the same sort of deliberate determination as we can raise up our socks? Perhaps this is why raising up the mind and heart tends to be replaced by 'responses', as this word underlines the call and response character of prayer and at the same time includes the notion of raising the mind.

Seeing prayer as a response leads us to understand that prayer consists as much in *listening* to God as in speaking to him (with or without words). Urs von Balthasar writes: 'Prayer is communication, in which God's word has the initiative and we, at first, are simply listeners. Consequently, what we have to do is, first, listen to God's word and then, through that word, learn how to answer'.

Again, in seeing prayer as a response there is place for those traditional characteristics of prayer listed as praise, love, repentance, thanksgiving, petition. For these are the normal reactions, one more pronounced than the others at any particular time, of one person to another who personally approaches us.

A further point needs to be made. The traditional description of 'raising the mind and heart' suggests that prayer is something that we do of ourselves, that when we turn to God in prayer we take the initiative. But this is not so. Prayer is a gift from God our Father. Prayer arises from his reaching out to us. God makes the first move by revealing himself to us and he invites us and enables us to respond to his self-communication. Prayer, then, is more correctly thought of as a response of the human spirit to God who addresses us. At the heart of all true prayer is the interplay of call from God and response from man.

The other traditional description of prayer as 'conversation with God' remains valid. This analogy well expresses the exchange in prayer which can be likened to a conversation between two persons. Nevertheless, what sort of conversation can be held with some one who is permanently invisible and silent? Consequently, 'communication' seems to be becoming preferred to conversation, since God is not a person as we are persons and he 'speaks' through various mediations: events, people, scripture.

Communication is the life-line of relationship. As God communicates with us in a variety of ways, so can we with him. Communication need not always be in words; it can also be by gesture and even by silence. The communication that is prayer need not be in a church or at any special time set aside for it. Man can pray at any time and in any place and create his own means of expression. So if the present younger generation tends to seek communication with God in ways differing from the past, we their elders must not be too hastily disturbed by the new forms, though we may reasonably advise them not to ignore entirely the valuable experience of the Christian centuries.

Prayer is sometimes spoken of as a 'spiritual exercise', as indeed it is. But the expression suggests that it is we who take the initiative rather than God. See what was said just above. Also 'exercise' does not adequately allow for the receptivity to the self-giving God that is so very important in prayer. That is why we find authors today bringing out this character by speaking of 'active passivity', which is by no means a contradiction in terms with regard to prayer.

We used to speak of 'methods of prayer'. This is legitimate, since one can work out different means to be used to obtain the end of prayer. But there is the very easy danger that method be exalted above the rank of a means or else that a person may cling too rigidly to one method. Freedom should be the mark of true prayer. There are as many ways of praying as there are pray-ers.

The traditional distinction between mental and vocal prayer is still regarded as valid and relevant. But we are advised to avoid a false dichotomy. They are not two separate types of prayer. Ordinary experience tells us that we do not speak without some thought, and that we do not think without some symbols, which are usually verbal symbols. The possible danger in separating them is that mental prayer may become a purely mental exercise and that vocal prayer degenerates into mere repetition of formulas.

To conclude. One need not be unduly disturbed by the changed attitudes towards prayer noted at the beginning. History of the prayer life of Christians could point to periodically changing patterns of prayer. The same Holy Spirit is guiding the people of God and he fosters variety.

F. SOMERVILLE

Situation prayer

Most Christians are finding prayer difficult in this secularized world. For many of them it has become a dead area. You can be quite sure that at retreats and religious discussions one invariable appeal is basically concerned with prayer today.

The kind of society in which we are living is secular; the 'secular city' is the accepted term since Harvey Cox's widely read book. A flood of literature continues to describe its many aspects. Here I do nothing more than pick out some features of this society which are unfavourable to the life of prayer, and also point to some others which are favourable if we know how to make use of them; then I shall be in a position to offer some advice on prayer today.

Unfavourable features

The majority of the population lack an explicit philosophy of life. Many of them go through life without any purposeful meaning. Life leads to death and that is the end. The characteristic is widely illustrated by our contemporary writers: it comes out clearly in current drama, novels and films. Moreover, in this society anyone can have and express his own opinion on any matter without any sort of inhibition. A man can belong to any church or none, church membership being regarded simply as a matter of taste. Society is neutral to all religious views. Atheism and agnosticism are as respectable as Christianity. Living with this background the good Christian has nagging doubts about a number of religious matters, and among them is the question whether prayer still has any meaning, since so many of his friends and acquaintances consider it a waste of time which would be better spent in active involvement in making the world a better place in which to live.

Another feature characteristic of the secular society in which men are rapidly learning to do everything for themselves is that God is ceasing to have a place in the world-picture of many people as he used to have. The time when belief in God was considered obvious is definitely gone. He was once thought of as Creator, Provider, stopper of gaps in man's knowledge and capacities. He is no longer any of that. Men can manage the world without him; they can forget him. God seems to be receding from the world.

What, then, is God? The theologians are now saying he is 'the ground of all beings'. But how do you pray to a ground? Can or may we address ourselves to God as a Person? If not, then prayer seems pointless. Many good Christians feel that the way they had been taught to pray — reciting prayers or meditating according to fixed patterns — means nothing to them now.

A further feature is that the secular city is technological. Its world is the object of man's mastery and manipulation. Life is a series of problems for which different kinds of specialists are trained and at hand to make experiments in order to produce results. The first question people tend to ask about anything is: does it work? In such a society they ask: what is the use of prayer? meaning: does it produce the goods? And when we think of our persistent prayers of petition we wonder.

Finally, as a result of technological man's achievement noise is incessant with the roar of traffic, the drone of factories and the flow of off-beat music. The pace of life is accelerated; whether you call this a merry-go-round or a rat-race, people have to rush from bed to work, from work to meals, and at the end of the day take a sedative before dropping into bed. We were once taught to set aside a certain amount of time each day for quiet prayer. But is there the quiet and the time in this day and age? How many people, outside monasteries, are able to enjoy the former peaceful rhythm of life?

Favourable features

People are absorbed in the tasks of this world and becoming more aware of their responsibility for it. They know this world. The 'other world', the 'world above', the 'supernatural world' about which religious ministers speak is nebulous, illusory, and certainly not as attention-catching as it may once have been.

This feature should help us to correct that two-world view which has prevailed for centuries. There are not two worlds, one in which we live and another in which God dwells. There is only this one world of ours. If we stop being other-worldly in our talk and stress this fact of one only world, we may help people to seek and meet God where he really is — in our own midst.

Many Christians are not yet fully aware of the immediate and constant reality of God in human life. He is with us every minute of the day. He pervades our life from within it. He speaks to us through the events of daily life and through persons. He is ever inviting us to respond to his self-giving. We can, then, reflect upon the interests and concerns of daily life to listen to what God may be saying through things, to discover his will, to act with love, to be thankful for what is good, to be sorry for what has gone wrong. Just as for Jesus who himself used ordinary human encounters and experiences as the occasion to reflect upon their real deep meaning, so for us the daily events of human experience are the matter and occasion of personal prayer.

Christians are so caught up in the tempo of modern life that they say they have not the time for prayer.

This difficulty which they experience should provide us with the opportunity to show that prayer is not a separate exercise, not some special department of life as we used perhaps to think; prayer is essentially continuous with all our activities. We can pray our life. In order to make the point we shall have to overcome that false antithesis between the secular and the sacred which is in their minds; we must lead them to see that these are not two distinct and separate areas, but that the sacred is at the heart of the secular.

People today show a deepened interest in the human person and a greater awareness of community. They attach great importance to personal relationships. They would not take God for real if he were simply a first cause or the necessary being, and not involved with persons.

This mentality opens the way to our emphasizing that prayer is precisely a matter of personal relations with God whom we meet in and through persons. We make friends and form communities because it is in our nature to love and be loved, and because communication with others is necessary for our human growth. It is in the personal dialogue that goes on that our strengths and weaknesses, likes and dislikes, hopes and frustrations come out, and we discover who we are, what we are, where we are going, how we get there. A similar process takes place in our prayer communication with God. Of course, we cannot prove this with objective arguments, since it is a matter of direct personal experience. All we can say is: test it and see for yourself. People, being more pragmatic nowadays, are not so much interested in theory as in practice.

This characteristic can be made use of by insisting that prayer is learned by praying. Spiritual guides are saying that it is much better to pray, however falteringly, than to read Grou, Rodriguez and the classic writers. And the best way to help another to pray is to share your own experience of prayer with him. We learn to pray by praying, at first in the company of one who is a pray-er, let us say a parent, then a teacher, then a kindred spirit or a group of kindred spirits. But only we ourselves form our prayer-relationship with God.

The practice of situation prayer

As regards the practice of prayer the conviction of God being in our midst constantly communicating himself to us through our lives, especially our contacts with others, should move us away from restricting prayer to those times when we deliberately withdraw from our daily routine to converse with him in church, chapel or bedroom. Since God is present to us in every life situation and since prayer is continuous with life, we have to see prayer as an activity much more rooted in daily life than we have been accustomed to do.

This conviction of God's nearness is the basis of the informal kind of prayer which may be called situation prayer as distinct from the formal prayer for which we withdraw from our usual occupations. Since all prayer is a response to God present and beckoning us, our basic attitude in life is to respond positively with the intention that his kingdom come on earth. Examining this basic attitude we find that it calls for effort in three fields. It means, first, reacting to all the successive situations, big and small, in which a man finds himself during the day. God 'speaks' in the human situation. Do I listen to him? How do I face up to the challenge contained in each situation of my daily round? Do I accept or reject the opportunity of the present moment?

Then, most of our time is spent with other people: God is present within every single one of them. To respect them is to respect God; to ill-treat them is almost a sacrilege. The kingdom of God is the union of the whole human family under his fatherly rule. Our Christian response to God means opening ourselves up to the people we meet, being ready to give of our time and energy to help them. Do I relate positively to people? When someone asks a favour, it is in a sense God who asks it. And when we grant it, we do it also for God, and God gives to that person through us. Finally, a special aspect of saying yes to people is to respond affirmatively to society. Whereas our personal relationships are mostly on the person to person level, we are also conscious of the solidarity of men and of our having duties to society. This means that we should try to influence for good the way society is formed and governed. Do I engage in some form of Christian social action on the local, national or international level? Or do I lack involvement in serving the needs of my fellowmen? The kingdom of God is not a heavenly Jerusalem, ready-made and awaiting us, but it is a city we are building up in partnership with God.

This co-operation with God within the human condition is not quite all for it to be accurately called prayer. At certain moments we explicitly turn to God and articulate this living response with a few words, like thy kingdom come, or all for you or yes, Father, or some such words which maintain the proper motivation of our actions.

We can carry this form of prayer a stage further. During most of our waking hours we are entertaining thoughts in our head, and in this process we are often talking to ourselves about ourselves. We are conducting a sort of inner dialogue with ourselves: I must put down the newspaper, I had better start off for work, I hope I don't have to wait long for that bus, have I got the fare. . . . It is possible to turn some of this into inner dialogue with God: Lord, it's time for me to put down the paper; Lord, I'm off to work; thank God the bus is on time; Lord, I hope the conductor doesn't mind changing a pound note; Lord, this woman beside me is taking up a lot of space, I wish she were less bulky and more attractive. . . .

We are at times confronted with a new or unexpected situation. We ask: Lord, what do I do now?

N

Of course, one will not be doing this every other minute. One will begin with only occasional comments and gradually increase the frequency according to temperament and desire. In practising this inner dialogue with God we shall find that we are becoming more aware of God's presence, more open to other people and more closely united with God here and now in Preston or Prestwich or wherever.

This practice is seen to be true prayer once we realize that God speaks to us through persons and daily events and that we respond to him in faith through these same persons and events.

The necessity of withdrawal prayer

Almost certainly the man who prays in the above manner will feel the need to take a short time off now and again for recollection. This means he will try to make time for prayer in the traditional sense of the word, prayer in withdrawal from immediate contact with neighbour and daily chores.

Indeed, I think that withdrawal prayer still remains necessary to the one who has found the liberation of situation prayer. Man must re-create himself from time to time in seclusion, not necessarily in a church, but in an armchair if this helps. We still need times of withdrawal in order to take stock, to ponder on what life is about, to look ahead to life-situations, to let sink in some encounter with God experienced in conversation with a neighbour, to ponder the gospels with a desire to be more like Christ. . . . Father Dalrymple, to whom I am indebted for much in this essay, puts it well in his book, *The Christian Affirmation,* 'In practice you can only pray all the time everywhere if you bother to pray some of the time somewhere'. And we remember that Jesus was very much taken up with the service of his fellow-men, but he made time to withdraw for prayer alone.

It is important that situation prayer should not exclude withdrawal prayer, a danger which threatens even priests and religious in the secular city. Most important of all is to keep them related: the situation prayer should precede (logically) and feed the withdrawal prayer, and withdrawal prayer must be grounded in the activity of every day life.

F. SOMERVILLE

The coming of Christ

The popular understanding of this

We say in the Creed 'he (Christ) will come again in glory to judge the living and the dead, and his kingdom will have no end'. Most of us put emphasis on that word 'again' and take the whole phrase to mean that Christ will come visibly a second time into the world, this time as judge. Indeed we commonly use the expression 'second coming' which, by the way, has no scriptural warrant. Writers and preachers are fond of contrasting the first and second visible comings of Christ, the first time as saviour, in lowliness and as a servant, the second time as judge and as universal king.

If we teachers take that line with our pupils, then, to quote the title of Richard Acland's well-known book, 'we teach them wrong'.

Grounds for this understanding

There is some excuse for this understanding by Christians. They point to a number of Jesus' parables in which he seems to predict a second coming, like the man who leaves his home for a long journey (Mk 13. 34s), the wicked husbandmen (Mk 12. 1s), the parable of the talents (Matt. 25. 14-30). In a number of his sayings Jesus seems to teach that he would come again as the glorified Son of Man. For example in the eschatalogical discourse that takes up all Matthew chapter 24 he combines prophecy on the destruction of Jerusalem with a description of the end of the world when the peoples of the earth will see the Son of Man coming on the clouds of heaven with power and great glory. In Luke 17. 22-37 we are given that part of this discourse which concerns the coming of the Son of Man. In Matthew 25. 34-46 Jesus' description of the last judgment contains a reference to his coming.

St Paul taught the coming of Christ as a future event. To the Thessalonians he writes of the great hope of God's people, the return from heaven of the risen Lord. They 'wait for his

Son from heaven, whom he raised from the dead, Jesus who delivers us from the wrath to come' (I Thess. 1. 10). Similarly, 'our commonwealth (i.e. real homeland) is in heaven, and from it we await a Saviour, the Lord Jesus Christ' (Phil. 32. 20). St Paul personally thought at some times that the return of Christ would be very soon, even in his own life time, and at other times that it would be long delayed. Both views are found expressed in his letters.

A misunderstanding

Yet the idea that Christ will certainly come again visibly amid stupendous astronomical portents to judge the living and the dead is a crude misunderstanding. We have taken imagery for literal fact. We have taken a literary device for plain truth. We have taken symbols as though they were literal predictions of an event which is to occur within the time process.

Jesus did not write the gospels; so we are not sure that he did actually say what is attributed to him. Consider the parables. The early Christians felt free to modify the parables of Jesus to make them fit their own present situation, and scholars have shown that the parables have come down to us in a form which reflects the concern of the Christian community waiting for the coming of the Lord, which they thought was near, rather than the situation in the ministry of Jesus. Dr J. Jeremias, the greatest of contemporary scholars on the parables, holds that most if not all of the 'waiting' parables had originally no reference to a second coming. We cannot draw a solid argument from the parables that Jesus taught a second visible coming on the last day. This conclusion is strengthened by the fact that the popular interpretation of the quoted parables (as well as the expression second coming) implies that Christ is absent from the world until he comes at the end. Yet this is completely contrary to the basic Christian belief that Christ is abidingly present in the world. With an absentee Christ Christianity is nothing.

Consider now the eschatological discourses. They contain apocalyptic elements with their cosmic disasters, earthquakes, solar eclipses and the rest. Such apocalyptic writing was not uncommon among the Jews; it was a literary device by which a writer commented on the present by means of an elaborate vision of the future with a wealth of imagery that is bizarre to us. We do not know how much Jesus himself drew upon the imagery of Jewish apocalyptic to spice his teaching. We do know he concentrated his preaching on proclaiming the kingdom of God for which he lived, suffered and died. Some of his sayings have been 'edited' by the evangelists, who like their contemporaries were expecting the parousia, that is the coming of Christ in the glory of his kingdom. This expectation inevitably influenced their thinking and writing. They had recourse to the Old Testament apocalyptic imagery, mainly Daniel 7. 13ss. 'Modern form criticism now shows that the eschatological discourse may be a compilation of sayings of Jesus like the sermon on the mount and thus need never have been delivered in the form in which it stands' (J. McKenzie, *Dictionary of the Bible*, s.v. parousia).

We have seen that Paul was in two minds about the 'return' of Christ. He saw arguments both for an early and a long delayed parousia. This is not surprising, because he was just as ignorant as any one of us. Jesus had said (and this is one passage which is admitted to be authentic since it is a confession of ignorance made by their Lord and so was hardly invented by the early Christians): 'But of that day or that hour no one knows, not even the angels in heaven, nor the Son, but only the Father' (Mk 13. 32).

But Paul was not in two minds about the 'coming' of Christ. He has many passages in his letters where he says that the coming of Christ will be in the future. He has many others in which he says that Christ has already come. And the two statements are quite compatible. The coming of Jesus Christ, who is man and Son of God, is, when you come to think of it, both historical and transcendental. Paul, like ourselves, can only think in terms of past, present and future and use symbolic language to express this religious truth. Jesus first came into the world at Bethlehem round about 6 A.D. In this sense Christ's coming is a past event. He accomplished the work the Father gave him to do. That work goes by many names, redemption being perhaps the most common today. But another name, also biblical, is the inauguration of a new creation. This new creation was made present with the resurrection of Christ. Christ is the principle of the new creation. If anyone is in Christ, he is a new

creature (2 Cor. 5. 7), a new man with a new life, sharing the
risen life of Christ, united with God in Christ. This new creation
is with us now. Christ comes daily into the lives of the baptized
and makes them sharers of God's life. We believe that he comes
into the lives of non-Christians also and draws them to the kingly
rule of God. He comes when we celebrate the liturgy, when two
or three gather in his name, when we perform an act of Christian
charity. In the most real sense the coming of Christ is a present
reality.

God's plan has been achieved with the resurrection of Christ,
but obviously his purpose cannot be brought to completion
until history has run its course and the end of the world arrives.
Looking at the abiding presence and activity of Christ from the
end of time (the last day), the early Christians were impelled
to speak of a final coming of Christ in the future.

The coming of Christ is a supernatural happening; it belongs
to the eternal order. It cannot be adequately described in human
language belonging to this present world-order; and this is why
Paul and ourselves are constrained to speak symbolically and talk
about a past, present and future coming. The final coming is
not a literal occurrence, but an image used to make vivid a
theological truth.

The real meaning

The words 'he will come again in glory' do not mean that
he will come once again, a 'second time', after having come
once before at the Incarnation. They are to be taken symbolically. The phrase stands for a present reality: Christ's abiding
presence and activity in the world. It also means that history
must come to a close with God's kingly rule fully established
and all things brought into a unity in Christ. Although the last
age of the world process has begun with the life, death and
resurrection of Jesus Christ, the end of God's purpose has not
yet completely come about, but we can confidently expect a final
state of the world when it will be completed.

It will be helpful to a right interpretation if we remember
that 'There is but one coming, begun at Christmas, perfected
on the cross, and continuing till all are included in it'
(J.A.T. Robinson, *Jesus and His Coming*, p. 185).

Catechetical notes

In the classroom we should give the real meaning of this article of the Creed. Some teachers may fear that this would do harm to the faith of the pupils. This is because they thmselves have long taken the scriptural passages as literal predictions of a future occurrence within the time-process. But the pupils will not be shocked. On the contrary they are shocked and incredulous at the fantastic things which are supposed to happen in the popular presentation of the doctrine — the cosmic upheavals, the raising of the dead, the appearing in the clouds with angels, the public parade of a last judgment. They are relieved to learn that these imaginary pictures were conjured up by ancient writers to impress an ancient people.

We do not in the least wish to take away belief in the final coming of Christ, in other words to do away with our article of the Creed. It must be retained, because although God's purpose in the Incarnation has been achieved with the death and resurrection of Christ it has not yet reached its final stage. Just as we teach that the kingdom of God has already come but is not yet fully established on earth, so we teach that the events of the Incarnation are already in action but the process of restoring all things in Christ is not yet completed. The idea of a final coming of Christ, as also of a last day, helps us to imagine the final completion.

Stress that the coming of Christ is a present reality. His coming means his abiding presence. Explain this in a concrete way. We see him coming in judgment whenever we have to make a personal choice in our dealings with our fellow men. We see his coming in power and glory in our own experience of personal renewal, whenever goodness prevails over evil. We see his coming in the growth of Christian virtues, conspicuously in the outstanding saints, but no less truly in the millions of ordinary Christians throughout the world who show a Christian character. We see his coming in the gradual growth of God's kingdom on earth despite the manifest evil. On this point the teacher will not identify the kingdom of God with the Church. The kingdom of God is his kingly rule in the hearts of men, and many non-Christians accept that rule.

J. P. WHELAN

The resurrection
of the body

The resurrection of Jesus leads us at some stage in our catechesis to consider that 'resurrection of the body' which we profess as part of our faith whenever we recite the Creed. The two truths are closely linked; for it is Christ's resurrection which gives us grounds for our conviction that we shall follow his way, that we shall 'be united with him in a resurrection like his' (Rom. 6. 5). Yet is there any teacher who has not experienced enormous difficulty in treating of our bodily resurrection? He is in good company here; for he will remember that the Greeks in Athens made mock of St Paul when he preached it before the Council of the Areopagus (Acts 17. 32). The Greeks believed in some survival after death, but this continuance was reserved to the soul, not to the body. Likewise, the Fathers of the Church met with the same resistance to the Christian teaching, a fact which accounts for the many efforts they made to find a rational expression and defence of a doctrine so uncongenial to the philosophers of their day. But I am here concerned with the Christian teacher today and how to help him in his difficult task of tackling this problem.

Difficulties to be faced

I think it is true to say that most adult Christians understand this doctrine to mean that at the last day our bodies will be re-united to our souls. At death, they have been taught, the soul is separated from the body and remains separated until the last judgment when God will somehow bring them together again. If they are Catholics they may even assert that we rise with the self-same bodies we had before.

Now this view is, to say the least, extraordinarily naive. No wonder it is utterly rejected by thoughtful people, both Christians and non-Christians. It raises unanswerable objections and difficulties, which lurk in the minds of even our Catholic pupils. How can a body be raised again when it has been eaten and assimilated by beasts and plants or has vanished into thin air at the blast of an H-bomb? Where is a soul between the moment of death and the final resurrection? How can a human soul exist on its own separated from the body? How will the body be re-united to the soul? What will our risen body be like? If you quote St Paul and say it will be a 'spiritual body', what does this contradiction in terms mean?

These are fair questions given the popular understanding of the doctrine; and they are unanswerable. The teacher has surely met them; he has felt uneasy and the pupils dissatisfied.

Things to be remembered

Perhaps the popular exposition of the doctrine is at fault. So it may help the teacher to set down some things which must be remembered when treating this difficult topic.

First, God has not foretold any details of what will happen to the individual after death. He has not given information about the future; he has spoken of eternal life and given promise of eternal union with him. We are, then, wasting our time if we search the scriptures for a clear picture of what is in store for the individual. The scriptures may represent in pictorial form God's revelation concerning our future, but this representation is not a literal prediction.

Secondly, we need to take the teaching of the New Testament as a whole and not fasten on to isolated texts. Individual texts were written in particular circumstances which need to be known for correct interpretation. This is particularly true of St Paul who is the writer most frequently quoted on this subject, and the one from whose language we have derived the phrase and the doctrine of the resurrection of the body. So the wisest course is to consider the evidence of the whole New Testament.

Since our belief in the final resurrection is biblical in origin the teacher must be careful in his interpretation of the scriptures. Thus the authors of the older text-books used to say that the doctrine of bodily resurrection was prepared in the Old Testament. They quoted Ezechiel 37. 1-14 (the coming to life of the dry bones), Isaiah 26. 19 (Israel's dead — not the pagans —

will be restored to the good life), Daniel 12. 2 (the resurrection
of the martyrs for the faith under Antiochus IV Epiphanes) and
2 Macc. 7 (the story of a mother and her seven sons who were
tortured to death rather than eat pork). But these texts do not
support the Christian belief of bodily resurrection. Ancient Israel
believed that the dead went to a place called Sheol where they
lived a dismal diminished sort of existence. When later the Old
Testament people came to think of deliverance from Sheol —
that is entertain some idea of resurrection — they understood
this as the revival of a corpse.

By the time of Jesus most Jews believed in a resurrection of
the dead. The exceptions were the conservative Sadducees. Jesus
seems to have sided with the majority opinion, as may be
inferred from his discussion with the Sadducees (Matt. 22. 23-33),
though he is cautious not to be specific about the nature of the
resurrection.

St Paul also believed in a final resurrection. About the year
50 A.D. he was telling the Thessalonians that the Christian
dead will rise at the coming of the Lord, although we cannot
tell what date this will be (1 Thess. 4. 16 and 5. 1). Five years
later he tells the Corinthians that the resurrected bodies would
not be the same flesh as the flesh which had been buried; they
will be very much changed (1 Cor. 15. 35-52). When he wrote
to them again at some unknown date, by which time he had
come to be convinced that he and his fellow Christians would
be dead before the coming of Christ, he says that the new
spiritual body already existed (2 Cor. 5. 1-8). Whether this new
body is an individual body, waiting in heaven, or, as is more
likely, the Church, the body of Christ, does not affect his
conviction of a resurrection.

When speaking of Paul's doctrine it is imperative to bear in
mind his view of human nature and the words he uses. For him
man is spirit, soul and body (1 Thess. 5. 23). For him spirit
(*pneuma*) is not strictly a part of man's make-up as such. It is
the Spirit of God which once came upon special individuals and
since Pentecost comes now upon all men; indeed it is so universal
and so close to each man's life that one can speak of 'my' or
'his' spirit. Soul for Paul corresponds to what we today would
call the *psyche*, that aspect of man which is studied by psychology. The term soul can also stand for the whole man. Body

for Paul is the whole man constituted by physical and mental relationships. It is not, then, simply the material part of man, as we have traditionally taken it to mean with our excessive and on the whole harmful distinction between body and soul. Finally, we may add the word 'flesh' (*sarx*) which Paul also uses. It corresponds to that aspect of man which is studied by the biologist. With Paul the word flesh could usually be used interchangeably with body in his sense.

The importance of remembering these terms of Paul is to bring home to ourselves the fact that we have used the words of this apostle without adopting his way of thinking. This accounts in large measure for the misunderstanding and the idle speculation with regard to the doctrine of bodily resurrection.

Thirdly, and most important to remember, is that our language about the resurrection of the body is and must be symbolic. When we speak of matters supernatural or transcending our spatio-temporal condition we cannot use words which adequately cover what we mean. All we can do is to have recourse to symbolic language, that is use language from ordinary human experience which points to something beyond our condition of living in space and time. In doing this we have to deny the natural meaning of the words but retain the positive reality pointed to. In general, all our religious language is and must be symbolic.

The importance of remembering this is that we shall not interpret the resurrection of the body as if it were an event in spatio-temporal experience. It is because they have lapsed into non-symbolic interpretations that many people in the past have held absurd views and conjured up false problems regarding this doctrine.

The meaning of the doctrine

We are now in a position to approach the meaning of the doctrine. That word 'resurrection' is used symbolically. Resurrection does not mean coming back to life or revival of a corpse. It stands for the transition from one mode of existence, in which we live under conditions of time and space, to a new mode in which these conditions no longer obtain. It is a transition from time to eternity.

Such resurrection is both present and future. If it were an event that was to take place only in the future, for example at the last day or after death, then we would know nothing about it, and we would have no hope; for we never hope for something about which we know nothing. Moreover, if it were simply a future event bearing no relation to our present experience, we would not be interested in it, because what we all want is, not the promise of 'pie in the sky when we die', but the assurance that our present life has some meaning and importance. Nor is resurrection something already present; for if this were the case we would have nothing to hope for; we would simply have to hold on to the present, which we know does not fully satisfy man. The very fact that man hopes for fulfilment and is never satisfied with his present achievement, shows that he is never in this world completely fulfilled.

Resurrection is, I repeat, both present and future. It is present in the sense that there is already an element of the eternal in man's experience. He experiences it particularly in moments of absorption in truly creative work and of deep love for another person and of deep prayer. These are moments when he seems to rise above the mundane level of everyday life and time ceases to have any real meaning. He feels that at such moments he is his best personal self. It is true that these moments pass; they cannot be held on to indefinitely; but they indicate that man does possess an eternal element within him so that talk of 'resurrection' is significant and relevant. Resurrection is taking place now; it is a transforming, enriching element in our life. To this philosophical consideration we must add the teaching of faith that resurrection begins at baptism when we are incorporated, i.e. enter into the body of Christ and become new men. The risen Christ, free from all limitations of time and space, yet retaining real continuity with his earthly life, lives in Christians and they in him. He is 'the heavenly man' (1 Cor. 15. 49), the man with the life of God. St John has Jesus saying that those who believe in him have eternal life and have already passed 'from death to life' (Jn 5. 24). They have eternal life here and now given by Jesus Christ. Eternal life is for the New Testament divine life.

Resurrection is also a future event. Man seeks personal fulfilment. He knows that all his actions throughout life are making him the person he will be, building up his destiny; but he also knows that true complete fulfilment, that ideal for which he hopes and which satisfies the eternal element within him, cannot be attained so long as he is living under conditions of time and space. He must experience some transformation by which he passes from temporal life to eternal life. But this transformation which brings personal fulfilment has not yet been reached; it lies in the future. Resurrection, the transition to a new mode of existence, is still to come. This accords with the teaching of faith which says that we shall all 'rise' at the last day. So the word resurrection is a biblical symbol for transformation and for saying that what was really dead can really be given a new life.

Let us now turn to that word 'body' in the phrase of the Creed. From what we have seen of St Paul's teaching, from whom Christians have borrowed the term, the body does not mean the material part of man, but the whole man. Resurrection of the body means resurrection of the person. This latter phrase might well be used in teaching so as to help obviate needless difficulties. In any case, the teacher should not perpetuate the contrast and separation between body and soul which has caused so much trouble in the past. Stress the unity of man: he is a living body, a bodily person, an ensouled body. The person will be 'raised'; the person will be transformed; the person will enter a new mode of existence.

The resurrection of the body means that the whole man will find fulfilment. Therefore it includes the material side of man's nature, and not merely the spiritual side or his soul, to use the old terminology.

Man is a person with and for others. His personal destiny is inextricably bound up with that of the human community. The biblical symbol of the resurrection of the body asserts that no individual can be saved apart from the whole of mankind. "*All* shall be made alive . . . we shall *all* be changed" (1 Cor. 15. 22, 51).

Man is organically linked through his body with all other life — of animals, the fish, the birds, the insects — and with all other matter in the universe. He is inescapably related to the whole of nature. Consequently the whole of the material world enters into man's eternal destiny. This is why some writers affirm that the biblical symbol of bodily resurrection includes the 'resurrection' of the material world. Perhaps this was in the mind of St Paul when he wrote: 'creation itself will be set free from its bondange to decay and obtain the glorious liberty of the children of God' (Rom. 8. 21). Correlatively, the same symbol expresses the truth that man's activity in this world as maker, technologist, consumer and citizen has an eternal significance.

C. G. ARMSTRONG